CINEMA OF THE FANTASTIC

CINEMA OF THE FANTASTIC

BY CHRIS STEINBRUNNER AND BURT GOLDBLATT

Saturday Review Press
New York

For Leslie

Acknowledgments

The authors wish to thank for their help Allan Asherman, Larry Casey, Elaine Chubb, Charles Collins, Jon Davison, Leonard Maltin, Mark Ricci, Steve Salley, Susan Stanwood, Neil Sullivan, and especially John Cocchi, who contributed so much information on the casts and credits of the films discussed.

Copyright © 1972 by Chris Steinbrunner and Burt Goldblatt

All rights reserved. No part of this work may be reproduced or transmitted in any form or by any means, electronic or mechanical, including photocopy, recording, or any information storage and retrieval system, without permission in writing from the publisher.

Published simultaneously in Canada by Doubleday Canada Ltd., Toronto.

Library of Congress Catalog Card Number: 76–154252

ISBN 0–8415–0183–1

Saturday Review Press
230 Park Avenue
New York, New York 10017

Printed in the United States of America

Design by Burt Goldblatt

CONTENTS

INTRODUCTORY NOTE

Fantasy is the imaginative force in man that releases him from ordinary existence and leads him through visionary worlds of either hope or dread. And fantasy in the cinema is as old as the cinema itself. It derives from a point of view that the movies embraced almost from the start. For film has managed across every decade of its life to express for audiences around the world man's fantastic speculations and nightmares.

The cinema of the fantastic has become a movie staple and is worthy of serious attention. It has grown from simple to complex. Sometimes its special effects have become highly technical, its landscapes totally alien; sometimes the landscape is no more alien than the twisted interior of a single mind. It has both cherished humanity and destroyed it. It has been both a shimmering vision of tomorrow and a dark warning. The cinema of the fantastic, in fact, embodies the meanings of a highly varied group of adjectives—bizarre, poetic, unearthly, satanic, haunting, horrific, imaginary (although an individual movie may not be all of these). Its essence is fantasy, though not in the Disney sense, and it ranges from fairy tales to monster movies.

In this book we have selected fifteen high points in the development of the fantastic cinema—fifteen fantasy films that illustrate, each somewhat differently, the imaginary worlds of man as portrayed by the motion picture. And the depiction of the fantastic began early. Our very first film, over half a century old, conducted its audience on what then must surely have seemed close to the ultimate voyage of the imagination: a trip to the moon.

Above all, it is an exploring cinema, mapping and conquering strange worlds. Together the fifteen motion pictures in this book form the geography of lands lost behind mists.

A TRIP TO THE MOON

In the airless, dusty valley bottoms of the moon, against a horizon of crater rims and rounded mountain ranges, the astronauts of today's pioneering lunar flights fulfill dreams centuries old, and in the cinema of the fantastic first woven, first dared seven decades ago, when the art of imprisoning images on celluloid was itself in a pioneer state. One of the first of such early attempts to capture the public imagination through the story film was a young Frenchman's wild account—at the very dawn of the age of cinema—of a journey by rocket from Earth to its orbiting neighbor.

The Frenchman was Georges Méliès, one of the most extraordinary figures of the late nineteenth century, whose skilled hands grasped all the intricate wonders of the new mechanical age but whose head was filled with fantasy. Born to a wealthy middle-class family, Méliès early demonstrated quick, agile fingers and was taught mechanics, construction, design, and drawing. A jack-of-all-trades, he soon began making his livelihood by all of these skills, but his extravagant imagination made him chafe against these pedestrian occupations. His dreams were full of elfin landscapes, impossible adventures, flights of magic beyond the bounds of

the ordinary. It was natural that such a youth should gravitate to the conjurer's art of magic . . . and to the greatest magician of his day, a man considered the father of modern magic: the legendary Robert-Houdin, whose theater was the talk of Paris.

Jean Eugène Robert-Houdin, who had been a notary's clerk but who, like Méliès, was lost to faraway enchantments, singlehandedly and determinedly brought magic out of the confines of conjuring tricks and mere sleight of hand into a higher realm of the art: elaborate stage presentations of dreams and nightmares and impossible worlds. His famous Théâtre Robert-Houdin in the Passage de l'Opéra presented entire evenings of magic. Traditional prestidigitation was followed by vast pantomimes with such titles as "Lost in a Harem" or "The Witch's Curse," intricate illusions involving often huge props, many people, and full stage sets. Robert-Houdin's trickery was on a level of spectacle and could take one anywhere from a sultan's court to a sorcerer's cave. Young Georges Méliès was drawn to it like a magnet to a lodestone, and he became Robert-Houdin's best follower. (Curiously enough, some years later in

America, a youngster named Ehrich Weiss, about to embark on his career as a magician, decided to compliment the man whose writings on magic had so inspired him by patterning his professional name after him: Houdini.)

In 1887, when he was twenty-six, Méliès purchased the Théâtre Robert-Houdin (Robert-Houdin having died some years before), settling down to what he imagined was a life's work: operating a showplace of magic. His ability in carpentry and mechanics soon enabled him to add new spectacle to the theater's repertory: demons appeared in bursts of flame, pretty girls vanished in smoke, massive goliaths loomed over their victims, suspended by cables or moved by men hidden inside. For eight years these wonders of the stage satisfied Méliès' creative spirit. And then he discovered the camera. All the fairies and the devils and disappearing ladies of his theatrical tableaux began to pale.

When Méliès saw his first motion picture demonstration in 1895, the new invention of "movies" had already caused a sensation in France and elsewhere. In Montmartre, at the Théâtre Optique in the Cabinet Fantastique of the Musée Grévin (still today the most mind-boggling waxworks museum in the world), Emile Reynaud was showing animated drawings in strips and mirrored drums, which when spun managed to string together action sequences that lasted several minutes. In America Thomas Edison had tried and failed to invent a "Kineto-phonograph," which he hoped would marry pictures to his already successful phonograph cylinder; by 1894 he had begun marketing the soundless Kinetoscope machine, which provided individual pictorial entertainment, in peep-show form, showing the viewer band drills and prizefights and vaudeville turns. But the film that Méliès was to see was the

The veritable father of the cinema of the fantastic, Georges Méliès. His Mephistophelian look makes it easy to believe that he featured sinister magicians and Satan himself in both his stage and screen extravaganzas.

4

enthusiastic creation of two brothers named Auguste and Louis Lumière.

The Lumières were both inventive photographers and astute businessmen. They were clever enough to realize that the best way to make pictures move was by pulling photographic strips across a light source by means of a claw, or sprocket, and visionary enough to guess the financial possibilities of such a machine. (Although the Lumières were not in fact the first inventors of a projector, they were the first to develop a really successful model.) By 1895 they had constructed and patented both a film camera for photographing upon perforated strips of film and a projector for showing them and had set up a screening theater in the basement of the Grand Café on the Boulevard des Capucines, charging one franc admission. The sharp realism of their scenes of French life astonished audiences: the splashing sea in which a bathing beauty frolicked seemed alive in its movement; a railway train hurtling into a station (and at the screen) caused spectators to faint. In a few months lines for the Lumière showings stretched through the district and two thousand people a day were marveling at the sights beneath the Grand Café. And in that audience was Georges Méliès, greatly excited over the possibilities of this new illusion for his magical shows. He must have the Lumière Cinématographe!

But the Lumière Brothers were determined to retain the process for themselves, even though Méliès offered them ten thousand francs for it. (The director of the Folies-Bergère offered fifty thousand, which was turned down as well.) Undeterred, Méliès vowed to build his own machine. After a trip to England to buy camera parts and film stock from another cinematographic pioneer, an optician named Robert W. Paul, Méliès in short order constructed a camera and a projector. At last he could add a new dimension to his theater of magic by photographing his most celebrated acts. He transcribed all his most visual and most baffling illusions onto film. Ladies vanished, to reappear stepping out of flame and smoke. Sorcerers escaped from their bonds and from locked trunks. He projected this film to his first audience, confident that the wonders of his stage illusions would make far more exciting screen fare than the Lumières' brief Paris vignettes, with their scenes of railway stations and factories.

To Méliès' complete surprise, his film was a failure.

It was merely a photographed magic act, with all the sense of immediacy gone. His audience was confused by the events on the screen, baffled by the mystery rather than caught up in it. Dismayed, Méliès experimented further and at the same time began using his camera out in the streets of Paris. It was on one of these open-air expeditions that a providential accident opened a whole new world for Méliès. He was photographing a busy Paris street—a bus lumbering by—when the primitive claw mechanism of his camera jammed, preventing the passage of the film. When he had finally cleared his locked gears and resumed filming, the bus had long since passed from sight. Later, viewing the footage he had shot, he was astonished to discover that the jamming of the film had seemingly transformed a bus into a hearse! This elemental bit of stop photography—for as his camera resumed shooting, a hearse was crossing the street where the bus had been—stumbled upon entirely by accident, taught Méliès that magic, rather than being set up outside the camera to be photographed, could be created within the camera. Could be created *by* the camera. The cinema of the fantastic was born.

Every wild visualization of impossible worlds, every soaring fancy of the camera's eye began in that Paris street. Méliès experimented further and soon discovered all the basics of trick photography. Speeding the action, slowing it down, or reversing it to make everything move backward, mingling real persons with miniatures, shooting indoors against realistic backdrops suggesting faraway places, ghostly shapes created by double-exposed film, multiple exposures enabling persons to talk to themselves on screen: all these devices were first developed by Méliès. His artful magician's brain was the perfect tool for creating film illusion, and for conceiving a film studio whose "stage" (Méliès had not lost his theatrical upbringing) featured a multitude of trapdoors, moving panels, and overhead pulleys to provide lightning entrances and exits by actors seemingly popping up out of the ground or descending out of the air.

For Georges Méliès was committed to fantasy. Nearly all the films he created over the next decade and more were spectacular flights of bizarre imagination, embracing every facet of the weird, the make-believe, the not-yet-happened. Demons and ghosts, high adventures and impossible travels, voyages to the bottom of the sea and the reaches of space, dreams and nightmares: all these Méliès explored, expanding and perfecting his photographic tricks and illusions.

Méliès' early subjects were extensions of ideas from his magical theater: short tales of besting Mephistopheles, of visiting the devil's manor or Merlin's lair, of humorous deliriums resulting from too much food and drink. But as Méliès perceived the ever-widening uses of his canvas, more epic themes came to his mind. He had read Jules Verne, and the possibilities of interplanetary voyaging intrigued him. The extremely visual idea of a projectile fired at the moon would make excellent cinema. Two years after the turn of the century Méliès' well-appointed, glass-roofed, electrically lighted studio in Montreuil began work on a project that would cost in excess of four thousand dollars—a voyage to the moon. It is the achievement for which Méliès is most remembered. And it blazed a trail for the fantastic cinema as well.

A Trip to the Moon (Le Voyage dans la Lune) was not, however, Méliès' first lunar vision. Four years earlier, in 1898, *The Astronomer's Dream* had a medieval court astronomer catch through his telescope the face in the moon mugging at him. The savant is joined on his balcony observation post by the king and his fool; he allows the royal eye to peer through the lens. The king sees a galaxy of stars; he observes Jupiter and Mars, and perched upon these planets are the gods for whom they were named. Training his telescope on the moon, the king surveys its live volcanoes, its mountain ranges, its snow. For Méliès, the terrain was later to be the scene of a large-scale landing, the first pictorialization of a rocket to the moon.

*A Trip to the Moon** opens with a group of French scientists, who look like wizards, disputing in a gabled astrolab. Their telescopes are pointed

---

*Although no official credits are extant for *A Trip to the Moon,* Méliès has left a record in a letter, dated 1930, of some of the performers. Méliès himself played the leader of the expedition (besides playing the lead, he wrote the scenario, directed and produced the film, designed the sets and costumes, and was in charge of the distribution.) Other actors included Victor André and two music-hall singers, Delpierre and Farjaux-Kelm-Brunnet. Bluette Bernon, another music-hall singer was the lady in the moon, while ballet girls of the Théâtre du Châtelet portrayed the stars. The moon imps, or Sélénites, were acrobats from the Folies-Bergère.

toward a polluted sky hanging heavy with the output of Paris factory chimneys. Theirs is a great undertaking. Soon they will be inside a massive projectile to be fired from a gargantuan cannon, and when blast-off day arrives, a carnival atmosphere surrounds the firing ground. A troupe of girls from the Folies, their music-hall costumes surprisingly similar to the hot-pants outfits of the 1970s, push the missile filled with scientist-astronauts into firing position within the cannon, then step back in parade formation to wave

the French flag and blow a salute on their trumpets. The immense cannon is swung so that it is aligned along the horizon toward the moon. The cannon is fired, and the projectile hurtles to the moon, shining brightly above cloud-decked peaks. Moments later the perilous flight is over. The landing is a deathless example of Méliès' peculiar whimsy: we see the globular, bloated face of the man in the moon express surprise at the object streaking toward it, and then—splat!—the missile has smashed into the face's left eye. A

A panorama of Méliès images, suggesting the range of his genius. In a carefully detailed sketch that he drew for one of his many films (upper left), a lab experiment goes awry, and a rubber head—a model of his own—bursts, for, as the caption states, too much passion can lead to catastrophe. Bottom pictures: Méliès as the captain in *Conquest of the Pole* and directing his actors in a historical play; a sketch of crustaceanlike moon people.

white lava substance—can it be overripe cheese?—exudes from the bruise.

The spacecraft lands in a rather cluttered crater, but to the astronauts who emerge from the ship the landscape is no fiercer than a rugged, stone-filled New World valley. Looking toward the horizon they see Earth rise like a ball rolling upward into the sky—an elaborate special effect for Méliès to attempt, and a remarkable forecast of the Apollo photographs of Earth made from the moon's rim. A small volcano erupts in the distance, mildly but prophetically, for science today is just beginning to believe in a volcanic moon. Perceiving that night is beginning on the moon, the travelers waste no time settling down for a nap, wrapping themselves in blankets and stretching out on the ground. Méliès had no concerns about the breathability of the atmosphere but

To the right, the frenzied preparations for a trip to the moon. The astronomers' telescopes focus on the polluted skyline of Paris. Pretty maids in shorts load the projectile, then snap to attention. At the bottom of the page, both versions—Méliès filmed this trip twice—of the spaceship slamming into the moon's surface. On the next page, bottom, astral deities float across the lunar heaven; top, an astronaut cuts up in *The Astronomer's Dream*.

had the foresight to cause a mild flurry of lunar dust, or snow, to cover the explorers as they sleep. Comets blaze past and celestial deities—ladies perched on constellations as in some mythological diorama—float across a star-filled heaven, peering down at the astronauts with amusement. Base camp is tranquil.

After the briefest of lunar nights our voyagers awake and begin an enthusiastic exploration of the crowded craters and peaks. They find their way into a moon cave, and in this secret world they discover wonders: gigantic mushrooms and other flora in a ground so fertile that even the umbrellas they have brought along, when planted, grow! Suddenly, the first citizen of the moon appears.

It is a moon imp: frail, something of a crustacean, his body and exposed ribs made of gritty shell, like a lobster's.

The invading earthmen are brought before the moon king, who is surrounded by his spear-carrying lobster guards.

(H. G. Wells' *First Men in the Moon,* published shortly before, proposed lunar inhabitants with somewhat similar structures. Méliès was clearly influenced.) The creature dances out at the explorers in a frenzied catapulting movement that might or might not be friendly. Throwing diplomacy to the winds, one scientist whacks at it with an umbrella, and the imp explodes into nothing. More appear and are similarly dispatched, but ultimately the astronauts are subdued and transported into the cave throne room of the moon king. It is a very ornate chamber, and the king, settling back amidst his elite guard of spear-carrying lobster soldiers, looks very much like some Moorish

emperor. The explorers make hesitant overtures toward interplanetary friendship, but His Majesty is suspicious and quarrelsome. So hostile does the confrontation become that one of the scientists, in a rather bellicose fashion and with little thought to the future of lunar relations, impetuously strikes at the king, who also vanishes into a puff of smoke. (Méliès' exploding people in this film were a special-effects stop-action feat so cleverly visual it really has not been bettered to this day.) In the confusion, our voyagers manage to escape.

Fleeing to the moon's surface, the astronauts retreat to their projectile. They push it to the edge of a cliff conveniently nearby and demonstrate Méliès' foggy but interesting ideas about weightlessness. All the scientists but one climb aboard the craft. The man remaining throws himself from the cliff, pulls the projectile down behind him by means of a rope, and the ship falls from the precipice into space. The heroic anchor man is of course hoisted inside.

In the film's final scenes the missile makes its return to Earth, plunging deep into a serene ocean, bobbing up again, and floating calmly until its inhabitants can be rescued by a passing three-masted ship. Méliès—as well as Verne—had a vision of the Pacific splashdowns to come.

This was not Méliès' solo spaceflight. In another, earlier, brilliantly hand-colored version of *A Trip to the Moon,* soldiers in plumed hats rather than cabaret girls load a projectile for a scientific lunar voyage. This time Méliès has the ship plunge into the *mouth* of a pastry-face moon; we see it land in the lunar mountains, and the emerging scientists are treated to a spectacular aurora borealis. Again, they settle down to sleep, but the weak crust of the moon's surface cannot support them, and they fall into caverns below. There they find the same amazing mushrooms but somewhat different denizens: polka-dot-dressed and nonigniting. A moon king, in polka-dots and crown, welcomes them, and a circle of pretty moon maidens breaks into a friendly dance. One of the scientists, aggressive in a romantic way, kidnaps one of the girls. This naturally angers the moonmen, and the astronauts hastily retreat to their ship—which, as in the other film, is pushed off a precipice to fall into space. Astonishingly, the missile on its return to Earth lands safely on the roof of the Academy of Science; the explorers gleefully present the kidnapped moon maiden to the surprised savants.

An echo rings across the valleys of the moon. The footsteps of people—you can almost hear them, against the crater-crusted horizons. The moon of the movies . . .

The mist-shrouded, ever-full moon whose rays drive men to love or to murder and change even those who say their prayers by night . . .

The moon that beckons us to it, inspiring rocket voyages, fanciful or accurate, from George Pal to Stanley Kubrick. Visionary voyages—to the moon, and beyond the moon to reaches outside our galaxy, from Flash Gordon to Captain Video to Barbarella to the starship *Enterprise* . . .

The lunar kings and queens, the hostile dwarfmen or catwomen of the moon, who eye us and our earth with sinister design, the colonized moon of *2001* . . .

All these voyages into space, these prophetic landings on the moon, these imaginary denizens owe their beginnings to that first space odyssey born in the small Montreuil studio with its magic-show trappings. The cinema of the moon began with Georges Méliès.

Méliès himself did not prosper, however. American mass-produced films, which drew crowds with their stars, had begun to push many small European producers out of the market. Others had discovered and were using Méliès' camera tricks. A more serious climate—the brink of world war—did not provide audiences for his style of whimsy. In 1914 his offices were taken over by the military, and Méliès disappeared.

Fourteen years later someone suddenly saw him selling newspapers in the street, an old and broken, but still proud man. He was bought a stand at a railroad station so that he could sell cigarettes and candy; finally, the Society of French Cinematographers—which he had helped to form long ago—found him a place in a home for impoverished actors. There he died in 1938, penniless. His funeral costs were paid for by English and French workers in the film industry.

But by the year of Georges Méliès' death the cinema of the fantastic had for decades been preparing mankind for reaching the moon. Already Fritz Lang's *Woman in the Moon,* a German film of the mid-twenties, had been uncannily accurate about the technical minutiae of launching a missile to the moon; *Flash Gordon* and *Buck Rogers* had already made rocket travel commonplace. In the years since, films have depicted—hopefully less prophetically—lunar battles, lunar invasions, even attempts by superior lunar mentalities to control the Earth. (Not to mention moonlit inspiration to romance and lycanthropy, to lovers and moon murderers.) The moon has always created in man a sense of wonder, but it was Méliès who first saw the globe's cinematic possibilities. It was the first giant step for the cinema of the fantastic.

METROPOLIS

Jon Fredersen	Alfred Abel
Maria/the Robot	Brigitte Helm
Freder	Gustav Fröhlich
Rotwang	Rudolf Klein-Rogge
Josephat	Theodor Loos
Number 7	Heinrich George

Directed by Fritz Lang
Story by Thea von Harbou
Cameraman: Karl Freund

A UFA Production, premiering in Berlin February 5, 1927

(In the United States release, by Paramount in 1927, Jon Fredersen has been renamed John Masterman, his son, Freder, has become Eric Masterman, and Maria is now Mary.)

For America in the 1920s, the cinema of the fantastic was of less importance than the cinema of the familiar. With far too few exceptions, the pleasant and the normal were extolled as the greatest of all possible conditions, and the hometown hero in his vine-covered cottage all too often reigned as a god. We were holding a mirror to ourselves; it was for us a time of carefree prosperity; we were a young, muscular world power, reckless and without a wrinkle of self-doubt. We needed fewer dreams—often bizarre nightmares that are the netherside of want—because of our accomplishments, our triumphs in the real world. The American cinema of the twenties was the cinema of achievement, of heroes overcoming all odds to claim monetary, status, and romantic prizes in a growing, prosperous nation. It was the confident, enthusiastic expression of the way we saw ourselves. The cinema of the fantastic needed other ground in which to grow. It found the fertility it required in the mood and outlook of a nation that had lost the world war, that had been drained of its youth and strength, that was struggling to free itself from national economic collapse. Germany, rife with stress and hopelessness, was ready for motion pictures of fantastic departures, fantastic solutions.

Two screen masterpieces made the German film industry the spokesman and innovator for the fantastic cinema of the twenties. The first, *The Cabinet of Dr. Caligari (Das Kabinett des Doktor Caligari),* was released in 1919. Its weird atmosphere and theme of insanity and murder became prototypes for later films in the German mode. In a traveling fair that has stopped at a small town, a somnambulist named Cesare—tall, thin-boned, with a deathlike face—rests in an upright coffin. Under the hypnotic command of his master, the terrifying Dr. Caligari, a squat old man with evil, piercing eyes, Cesare answers while in deep sleep questions about the future. A young student named Francis and his friend Alan attend the fair; Alan asks how long he has yet to live, and the somnambulist answers, "Until dawn." That morning Alan is stabbed to death by an unknown murderer.

Francis is certain Cesare is the killer, but no one will believe him. He begins to haunt the carnival grounds, watching Caligari's tent, where Cesare rests inside his cabinet. It is a nightmare vigil, and the surrealist mood of the film grows. It takes some time for Francis to discover that the body within the coffin is a dummy and that the real Cesare is roaming the countryside, commanded by his master to perform evil deeds. One of them is the kidnapping of Francis's girl, Jane. This was the first popular use of one of the most enduring of horror film images, that of the monster stumbling away with the terrified heroine swooning in his arms. Ultimately, Francis traces Cesare to an insane asylum, where to

his surprise he discovers Caligari to be the director! From the doctor's papers, he learns that Caligari has become obsessed with an eighteenth-century legend about a traveling somnambulist who kills under hypnosis—and tries to make the authorities aware of this. But at the end we discover that we have been inside Francis's nightmares, that Francis, Jane, and Cesare are all lunatics in the asylum, watched over and treated by a mild and friendly Director Caligari.

The second film masterpiece to arise from Germany's exploration of the fantastic was a peculiarly Gothic vision of Bram Stoker's *Dracula,* retitled *Nosferatu,* in order to escape paying royalties. The pleasant Victorian interludes of the book have vanished, and Nosferatu has lost all of Count Dracula's cultured veneer, becoming instead almost total monster, evil visible like a corruption in his face. When he darts from his Carpathian homeland to the German port city of Bremen—he has bought a house there from the unfortunate hero, who becomes his slave—he brings with him hordes of rats, spreading pestilence and death. Actually, with his erratic movements and corpselike face, Nosferatu (frighteningly portrayed by Max Schreck, whose last name is the German word for *fright*) resembles a giant cloaked rat. His evil spreads like a plague in the city, until he is stopped by the self-sacrifice of a force for good, the hero's wife, and disappears into dust in the first light of the sun.

At once, Germany's fantastic cinema drew international attention. Films like *The Golem (Der Golem,* 1920) and *Waxworks (Wachsfigurenkabinett,* 1924), names like Caligari and Cesare—and the actors who played these roles, Werner Krauss and Conrad Veidt—became known beyond the borders of Europe. (Veidt in particular devoted much of his career to macabre roles, ultimately bringing his talents to the United States in 1940 for the filming of *The Thief of Bagdad,* in which he portrayed Jaffar, the evil grand vizier.) In America, *Caligari* and *Nosferatu* were especially influential, in many ways the proto-models for *Frankenstein* and *Dracula* and their descendants released by that most Teutonic of United States studios, Universal, then headed by the German-born film pioneer Carl Laemmle.

One of the bright, innovative young directors to emerge from Germany's new studios was an Austrian youth who had started writing some thrillers for the screen and seemed competent to direct as well; his name was Fritz Lang. The screenplays Lang had written, often in collaboration with his new wife, the dynamic young Thea von Harbou, often dealt with the supercriminal (a figure Lang was to return to again and again) and with exotic adventures in faraway lands. His first directorial success, in 1921, was a brooding, able addition to the cinema of the fantastic. *Tired Death (Der Müde Tod)* tells of a young girl who tries to bargain with Death for the life of her departed lover; Death takes her through three past ages: Bagdad in the time of the *Arabian Nights,* a street carnival in seventeenth-century Venice, and ancient China at the court of the emperor. She meets her lover in all three settings and loses him in all three to the Stranger, Death. Ultimately Death offers to spare the boy in exchange for someone else's life; the girl pleads with the elderly persons in her village, but none will sacrifice himself. Then the girl spies a baby in a burning house; surely this can be a sacrificial offering. But she cannot bring herself to let the baby die. She rescues the child and dies herself in the flames—to find her lover waiting for her beyond the rim of Death.

The film, with its three tales of the contest between love and death against romantic, fantastic settings, was a great success both in Germany and abroad, and Lang was hailed as an important new director with a flair for weird and unusual themes. He chose his next project with care: it was a massive thriller, done in two feature-length parts, about an incredible criminal mastermind—*Dr. Mabuse, der Spieler* (1922). *Spieler* means "gambler" in German, but a literal translation does not fully convey Lang's wider meaning. Mabuse the madman gambles, unseen, with the destinies of countless lives and even the fate of a nation. He is often in disguise, portraying several personages in turn, constantly spinning his webs to entrap weak, unwary victims in the clubs, cabarets, seance chambers, and dark alleys of a Germany increasingly given over to decadence and lawlessness.

In Mabuse, Lang elevated the supercriminal to olympic heights—and curiously pitted him against the plodding public prosecutor, Wenk, a seeming bureaucratic workhorse who is clearly no competition for Mabuse. But in the end destiny—Mabuse's real adversary—is on Wenk's side, and despite attempts by the archcriminal to kill Wenk with a bomb and later to hypnotize him into destroying himself, the prosecutor manages not only to survive but to ferret out Mabuse's secret headquarters, to which he leads a large squad of police. His gangs of thieves and murderers caught, his empire collapsing about him, Mabuse goes mad: the ghostly faces of his victims appear before him, as he turns into a gibbering idiot. Wenk finds him in this condition, and Mabuse spends the rest of his days in a madhouse, endlessly charting on bits of paper schemes to conquer society.

The film was a runaway success. More than a decade after World War II,

Lang, who had left Germany in the early thirties, was invited back to that country to help revitalize its film industry, and, in 1960, he completed an updated but still familiar Mabuse thriller called *The Thousand Eyes of Dr. Mabuse (Die Tausend Augen des Dr. Mabuse),* in which at one point a clairvoyant at a seance moans, "I see dark clouds . . . I see *murder!"* This film in turn inspired more than a half dozen Mabuse sequels tackled in fast-moving fashion by lesser German directors.

Lang's next project after *Dr. Mabuse* was even more sweeping: *Die Nibelungen,* a two-part version, each part feature-length, of the nation's most cherished legend, the story of the victories and death of the folk hero Siegfried. Although Lang had dealt with period fantasy in *Die Müde Tod,* his involvement with Siegfried confronted him with an environment that included dwarfs and dragons, clashing swords and pagan courts. Siegfried is ultimately vulnerable because, while bathing in dragon's blood, one small part of his skin is covered with a fallen leaf and left unprotected. He is killed, and his beloved Kriemhild executes a bloody revenge. It is an epic of particularly German appeal, and Lang did both its spectacle and blacker moods full justice.

The worldwide popularity and financial returns of the Siegfried films guaranteed Lang a free hand in the choice of his next subject. But for Lang it was a difficult choice: he was flamboyant enough to realize he had to progress beyond supercriminal melodramas and historical sagas to ever larger, more arresting themes. But what direction would such a theme take?

Late in 1924, Lang joined other German film notables in a visit to the United States for a firsthand exploration of American studios; a

In Metropolis, the city of the future, society's elite frolic in lush gardens cultivated high above the machines that actually run the city. Freder, son of the ruler of Metropolis, indulges in some of the city's pleasures amid the splashing fountains.

18

transatlantic crossing via luxury ocean liner was then a very popular German pastime. Standing on deck as the skyline of New York City spread before him, the geometric towers ablaze with a galaxy of lights against the gathering dusk, Lang—impressed, like all European travelers, with a city such as the Old World has never seen—was seized by speculation about the future of this twentieth-century colossus. How would all this might, this vital mingling of steel and humanity, expand into the year 2000? Lang began making notes; he had found the subject of his next film project.

The next year work was begun on the most ambitious—and ruinously expensive—motion picture Berlin's UFA (Universum Film A.G.) studios had ever attempted. At a time when science fiction was not as yet a screen category, Fritz Lang began an epic portrait of the city of tomorrow.

As *Metropolis* opens, we see a great city of the far future, complex built upon complex, the sky nearly blotted out by multilevel architecture stretching as far heavenward as the eye can scan. Across this futuristic horizon dart small aircraft and helicopters, among myriad floating *autobahnen* spanned between massive buildings. It is an incredible, visionary spectacle. (The tabletop models were months in the construction and covered nearly an entire fair-sized UFA studio stage.)

Two of *Metropolis's* most enduring images—the hapless worker moving the levers on a giant dial, and the massive underground powerhouse, about to change, in Freder's vision, to the face of Moloch.

We are introduced first to the workers, uniformed identically in prisonlike garb and quartered far below the city's cosmopolitan surface. Like sleepwalkers they move in slow cadence when their shift is done to the elevator shafts that carry them down to their ·drab underground housing, while another elevator disgorges a new shift of workers, also marching in somnambulist steps.

Meanwhile, high above even the surface streets of upper Metropolis, the sons and daughters of the rich frolic amid the fountains and peacocks of lush pleasure gardens. One of these is Freder, young aristocrat of the year 2000, son of the Master Industrialist of Metropolis—and a sensitive youth. As

he laughs and sports, a girl suddenly enters the garden, leading a small group of ragged children. The girl is blond, beautiful, yet almost saintly-looking, with faraway, poignant eyes. "These—these are your brothers," she says. Staff members quickly usher her out; she is only a worker's daughter. But Freder has already been smitten. The girl's beauty and what she has said disturb him. Previously he has never thought of the workers, or of the huge machines that run the city from far below. Now a voice within him insists that he at least see the workers' domain, a world as remote from his as Mars might be.

No doors are forbidden to Freder, Jon Fredersen's son. He makes his way down to the level of the machines: incredibly huge pistons, dynamos, furnaces, stretching as far as one can see. The massive control center is a complex of machinery as high as a mountain, with an army of workers swarming over its sides like ants, regulating its dials and levers. But the giant machinery seems to be driven with a fury beyond human controlling. Suddenly one exhausted worker falls back, unable to keep up with the ever-changing dials. Pressure builds and the mammoth boilers at the machine's feet burst. Scalding steam shoots up the sides of the monster, screaming workers fall from their levels, and even Freder—some distance away—is knocked down by the shock vibrations.

Stumbling to his feet, the young man has a momentary hallucination that the vast multileveled machine, its furnace blazing and great clouds of steam obscuring its face, is actually Moloch, the monster of antiquity, consuming humanity. As Freder watches, he thinks he sees row upon row of workers move in procession into Moloch's yawning mouth to sacrifice themselves.

Agitated, Freder rushes to the office of his father, high above the city itself. The elder Fredersen is unimpressed; accidents such as his son has witnessed are unavoidable. "Why did you go down into the machine rooms?" Freder remains tremendously shaken: the workers are his brothers, he moans, repeating the word used by the blond

Below, the Tower of Babel, and the men who conceived it, without concern for the workers who must build it. At right, the scientist Rotwang reveals his robot woman to the ruler of Metropolis. Note his metal hand.

girl. "It was their hands which built this city of ours, Father! But where are these hands in your scheme?" The Master of Metropolis turns cold eyes toward his son: "In their place—*in the depths.*"

Rebuked by his father's sternness and heavy at heart, Freder makes one more trip down to the level of the machines. There in the smoky underground he witnesses a worker falter as he manipulates the levers of a gigantic dial, like the hands of a great clock. The workman falls, and Freder takes his place at the machines, moving the massive "hands" from one to another connection point. It is a hard task.

Meanwhile Freder's father has descended to one of the shadowy quarters of the surface city, to a dark old house still constructed along old-fashioned, nineteenth-century lines. It is the home of Rotwang, a scientist and an evil man, with one metal hand and a dwarf servant. His eyes blazing, Rotwang hisses at Fredersen: "I have created a machine in the image of man that never tires or makes a mistake! Now we have no further use for living workers." Entering the dark laboratory, sidestepping its coiled wires and electronic devices, the Master of Metropolis sees a figure in metal, its molded parts shaped to resemble a woman's face and body, erect on an electricity-charged throne. On a silent signal from Rotwang, the figure

stands . . . and walks . . . and holds out a hand to Fredersen, a metal hand strangely like the one worn by the scientist. Rotwang waves his metallic fingers in the air: "Isn't it worth the loss of a hand to have created the workers of the future—the *machine* men?" Another day's labor and he will have created a robot indistinguishable from a human being.

But this is not what has brought Fredersen to the scientist's home. For months now foremen have been bringing the ruler of Metropolis pieces of paper with designs on them found in the workers' clothing. What can the designs mean? "As usual, I come to you, Rotwang, when my experts fail me." The scientist studies the markings for a long time. "These are the plans of the ancient catacombs—far below the lowest levels of the workers' city." What is down there to interest the workers, Fredersen muses. Without a word, Rotwang hands him a powerful flashlight, gives himself one, and points to a stone stairwell leading downward into darkness.

In the machine rooms, an exhausted young Freder has taken the place of the fallen worker—he has even donned a uniform and numbered cap—at the giant dial for the remainder of the shift. Moving the heavy dial levers from one position to another is a job tougher than any Freder has ever done, and the ten hours of his shift are an agony. He weeps for pain when the changeover whistle blows, and collapses. But the fellow who helps him up whispers in his ear, *"She* has called another meeting." Freder stumbles after a group of silent workmen descending dark passages to a still lower level. They enter a sort of stone assembly chamber. Freder looks up, and there, before an altar of candles and crosses, stands the beautiful blond girl of the pleasure garden.

"Today I will tell you the story of the Tower of Babel," her soft voice begins. In ancient times, she relates, a great tower was planned, whose summit would touch the skies, and thousands were hired to build it. Alas, the toilers knew nothing of the dreams of those who had conceived of the tower, who cared nothing for those who were building it. The hymns of praise of the few became the curses of the many, and ultimately each side turned upon the other, and the tower fell. "Between the brain that plans and the hands that build, there must be a mediator. It is the heart that must bring about an understanding between them," the girl exhorts. "Maria!" the crowd of workers shouts, and she leads them in prayer. The men fall to their knees.

From a concealed spy hole Fredersen and Rotwang watch the scene below anxiously. The Master of Metropolis turns to the scientist: "Rotwang, make your robot in the likeness of that girl." As the scientist nods in agreement, Fredersen continues, "Hide the girl in your house, and I will send the robot down to sow discord among the workers and destroy their confidence in her." The industrialist storms out of the workers' world and back into his.

Below, her sermon finished, Maria dismisses her congregation. One figure remains behind: Freder. She recognizes him from that afternoon in the pleasure garden, and they touch. The young man's sensitivity and his feelings for Maria's cause kindle an instant response—very much like love at first sight. They kiss and agree to meet again tomorrow in the cathedral in the surface city. Freder and Maria part; candle in hand, the girl walks farther into the tunnels of the catacombs. Suddenly she senses someone following her. She hurries faster, but the pursuer stays close behind. She drops her candle, which still burns where it falls; a metal hand snuffs it out. The strong beam of a flashlight tracks her; she finds herself in a rockbound cul-de-sac.

In the cathedral Freder searches for Maria the following day; she is nowhere. He pauses before a particularly grotesque Gothic sculpture of the seven deadly sins, shakes his head in bewilderment, and walks aimlessly, despairingly through the darker byways of the city.

Before a strange, oddly shaped dark house with an astrologer's star on the door, Freder hears a scream—Maria's scream. (The house is of course Rotwang's.) He bursts through the door, darts through many narrow passages and book-lined rooms. Below, in Rotwang's secret laboratory, the scientist's metal hand has already stifled Maria's cries and pulled the levers that have begun the process of transforming his robot into the girl's image. Transformers bristle. The figure shimmers with electric halos. Unaware of this, Freder wanders into the streets once more.

In the spacious office of the Master of Metropolis, Rotwang proudly presents his achievement: an exact mechanical likeness of Maria. The elder Fredersen notes that the copy is perfect. "Now go down to the workers and undo Maria's teaching; stir them up to criminal acts." The robot winks one dark-rimmed eye and, leering evilly, embraces him. Freder bursts through the door. *"Maria!"* he cries out. Events have been too much for him. He collapses to the ground.

He is in a fever for days. Rotwang demonstrates his robot at a reception for Metropolis's most important citizens: in his delirium Freder imagines a voluptuous, lustful Maria dancing obscenely before an audience barely able to hold themselves back. Freder sees the figure of Death, who leads the seven deadly sins in the cathedral sculpture, come to life and swing his scythe through the city streets. While Freder lies weak and helpless, the robot Maria inflames the workers below the

streets. "I have preached patience . . . but your mediator has not come—and will never come!" The words do not fall on deaf ears. "Why should you sweat yourselves to death for the lord of Metropolis? Who keeps the machines going?" She whips her audience to a wild pitch. "Let the machines stop. *Destroy the machines!"*

A weakened Freder has just made his way down to the catacombs when a stream of workers, now in full revolt, pushes him aside like a piece of kindling wood. An exhorting, triumphant Maria—one imperfect robot eye beginning to squint grotesquely—leads an army of workers to the level of the machines. "Are you mad?" cries a bearded, burly foreman to the mob. "If you destroy the powerhouse, your own homes will be flooded below!" But the mob will not be stopped. It cheers lustily as the robot Maria starts the great dynamo spinning faster, faster . . . the power dynamo sparks off great bolts of lightning, and explodes.

In the intervening time the real Maria has made her escape from Rotwang's laboratory and has fled down to what she thinks is the safety of the workers' city. But the great drab square is empty. Suddenly a geyser of water bursts through the pavement, and great waves force their way through new cracks in walls and ceilings. The massive water tanks of the generators of the machinery level above have broken open. Maria sees a child trying to escape the rushing tide flooding the streets—and more children dart from doorways. Fighting down her own fear, she tries to lead the children to the safety of higher ground. But the workers' city itself is doomed. The buildings are starting to collapse. Only the great open square seems safe. And in the elevated center of that square, now crowded with children, is a great circular bronze gong. Maria begins to

25

The most important citizens of Metropolis gather at a glittering reception to watch the robot Maria dance. At first she appears as a goddess wearing a jewel-encrusted headdress, but as she begins to dance, the lights playing against and behind her reveal the underlying eroticism of her movements. Fritz Lang turns his camera to the watching men in their stiff formal clothes. The sexual intent of the dancer is not lost on them. Their lust is openly shown.

sound the alarm, to warn everyone who
may yet be in the crumbling, flooding
city.

Freder, making his way out of the
catacombs, hears the alarm; it leads him
to the square and to Maria. "Quickly!"
he cries. "The reservoirs are broken! We
must get up to the higher levels!"

But all is chaos.

In his office, high above the highest
level of Metropolis, Jon Fredersen hears
of the destruction of the machine
rooms, the flooding of the underground
city. "Where is my son?" he moans, as
below him the myriad streets go dark
and everything comes to a powerless
standstill. A solemn underling tells him,
"Tomorrow thousands will ask that
question."

In the ruined powerhouse, before the
smoking wreckage of the dynamo,
berserk bands of workers dance hand in
hand. The bearded foreman struggles to
get their attention. "Your city is
destroyed," he cries, "your children are
all drowned!" The giddy hysteria of the
crowd turns solemn and sullen. "It's
the girl who's led you to this! Kill her!"

Even on the surface streets of
Metropolis, crazed crowds in
fashionable evening dress dance and
drink and loot, in the collective
realization that their way of life is
doomed. Heading and orchestrating this
madness, and held aloft by the dancers,
is the robot Maria. A mob of workers
who have raged up to the surface level
spot her, however, and seize her for
themselves. A great pyre of debris is
collected in the cathedral square, and a
laughing, shrieking Maria is tied to a
post in its center. The wreckage is set
ablaze. As the flames lick at the robot
girl, she still laughs mockingly. . . .

Freder and the real Maria have made
their way, with the children, to the
safety of the surface level, but they
have been separated as the mob swirls
about them. Maria, frightened, seeks
refuge in the now empty cathedral—and

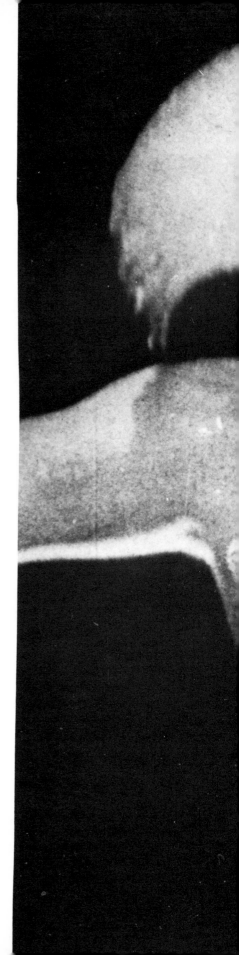

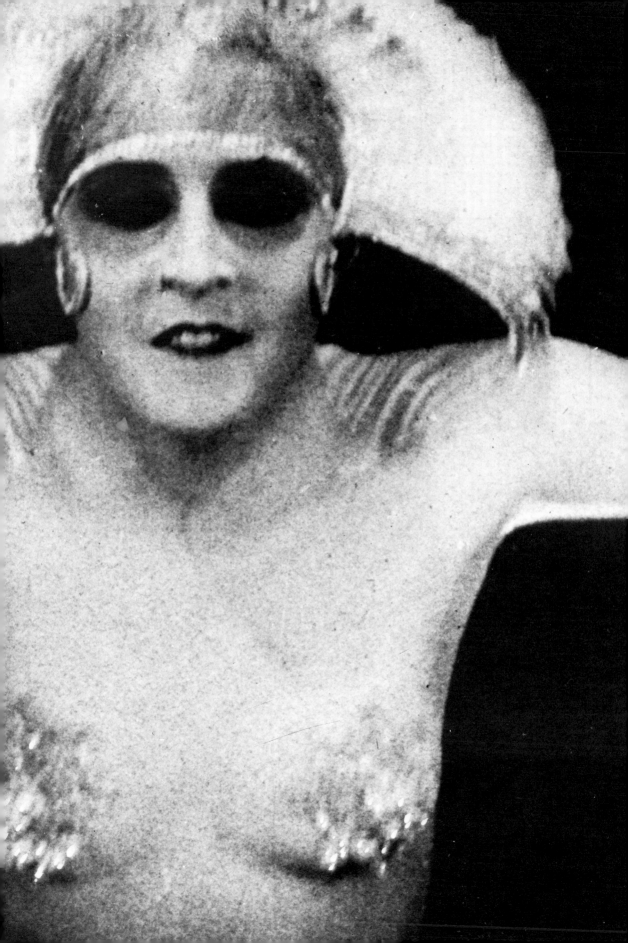

suddenly sees the dark figure of her recent captor, Rotwang. And the scientist sees her. If the mob outside learns there is a second Maria, thinks Rotwang, they will kill him for having deceived them. Seizing the girl, he closes his metal hand around her throat, but she breaks away.

Meanwhile Freder has come upon the pyre and, in despair, thinks it is Maria who is burning at the post. One more look, though, and he sees that the flames have eaten through the skin to the mechanical framework beneath. Then he hears a scream from the roof of the great church. It is Maria—with Rotwang! He rushes up to the cupola. The girl has managed to evade the scientist's grasp, and Freder attacks him furiously. They struggle on the dangerously narrow roofing. The scientist loses his balance and falls to the pavement far below.

When Freder and Maria descend, there is a massive confrontation in the cathedral square. The now sober workers have been told that it was Jon Fredersen's son who saved their children. The master industrialist of Metropolis is there himself, in equally

In the central square of the workers' underground city, the real Maria sounds a warning to its inhabitants that their subterranean homes are doomed. Already the square is flooding, and the children whom Maria has alerted are seeking the safety of higher ground. Behind, we see some of their drab dwellings, a grim underground world ripe for destruction.

sober mood. Maria and his son approach him. "There can be no understanding between the hand and the brain unless the heart acts as mediator," she pleads. Hesitatingly, the aristocratic master of the crippled city and the burly, bearded foreman reach out and clasp hands. A beaming Maria and Freder embrace. Together, all together—hand, heart, and brain—they will rebuild Metropolis.

Metropolis attracted international attention, and audiences formed long lines at box offices in many countries. Acclaim was not universal, however. While no one questioned Lang's imaginative genius, many critics were more than mildly disturbed by the ruthlessness and battle lines of his future society—a chilling glimpse, some felt, of the ultimate realities toward which Germany's political enthusiasms might be leading her. And the film was not the financial success everyone had hoped it would be. The making of it had been so long and costly that UFA had had to borrow heavily, even from American studios. Although money began to pour in after the film's premiere, it was just not enough: the proud German studio was dangerously close to bankrupcy. Finally it was sold, and much of the leadership that had guided UFA to its early success was swept from positions of power. The new owner was a publisher and a member of the National Socialist party.

Fritz Lang wisely chose a less epic spectacle for his next UFA film (1928). *Spies (Spione)* is a thriller with the familiar master criminal operating under a variety of identities, but in such realistic settings as large banks and government buildings. Following this melodrama, Lang embarked on his last futuristic project: *The Woman in the Moon (Die Frau im Mond).* The film begins with an extremely accurate depiction of a rocket preparing for

launching on a lunar voyage; it is expected that gold will be found on the moon. Lang intriguingly forecasts that one of the astronauts will be a woman; alas, once the crew (and a stowaway boy) have landed on the lunar surface a love triangle and plain greed interfere with any larger steps for mankind.

Lang entered the sound era in 1931 with *M,* a classic study of a twisted murderer of children moving with roving eye through an ordinary German town. It was to bring new success to the director and instant fame to his star and discovery, Peter Lorre. Feeling at home with the crime film, Lang turned once again to an old friend, the master criminal, and prepared *The Testament of Dr. Mabuse (Das Testament des Dr. Mabuse)* for release in 1933. From behind the bars of the madhouse in which he has been placed, the insane Mabuse plots the destruction of society, and when Mabuse himself dies, the director of the asylum becomes obsessed with the plans the fiend has left behind. The film offended Propaganda Minister Goebbels, and the film was banned and nearly all prints destroyed. Although Lang was still on speaking terms with Goebbels—indeed, the latter even offered him a job making government films—the director thought the political climate would soon become unhealthy. So, the very day of the offer from Goebbels, and smuggling with him a single print of *Testament,* Fritz Lang left Germany.

(There are conflicting reports about what really displeased Goebbels in *The Testament of Dr. Mabuse.* Many claim the script and feeling of the film were anti-Fascist, yet it was written by Lang's wife, Thea von Harbou, who was already an ardent Nazi, and who would not accompany Lang in his exodus. Paul M. Jensen, in his excellent study *The Cinema of Fritz Lang,* suggests Goebbels wanted a Führer type to be the one to destroy Dr. Mabuse's corrupting forces at the film's climax, but Lang refused.)

Lang eventually made his way to Hollywood and a long, distinguished career specializing in crime and spy melodramas, bringing critical and artistic notice to an often neglected category of film. He adapted easily to Hollywood's directorial styles and to the American idiom—even though his films often hinted of darker shadows cast across older streets . . . and older evils. The master criminal, less powerful in his unfamiliar American quarters, nonetheless emigrated with Lang and still lurked wraithlike in many of his American films. However, Fritz Lang was never again to pay cinematic homage to the city of the future.

UFA and its studios—where the streets and levels of Metropolis had first been charted and built—during the war became a mere Nazi tool, churning out simple musicals and propaganda features. With the bombing of Berlin, UFA itself was virtually destroyed. After the war, the German film industry rebuilt its studios far from Berlin, choosing as a more convenient location the outskirts of Munich. UFA was finished.

And yet the marvels of the Metropolis it had introduced to the screen were not to fade. As the prototype futuristic city, however, this 1926 model was in some ways flawed. Rotwang, for instance, as a scientist, looking like a wild medieval wizard, with occult symbols cluttering his crooked, ancient house, would be unthinkable in the twenty-first-century world of Jon Fredersen, as his inventions would be. A real Rotwang,

scientist of Metropolis, would not bother with robot Marias, or even robot workers, but would go straight to the heart of the problem and create *robot machines*. The automated, computer-brained, self-perpetuating machines of the future would be the ones to revolt against and destroy Metropolis's ordered, upper world, without a single clenched human fist or worker's cry of vengeance. As for Lang's workers themselves—stylized, anonymous, collective, moving like sleepwalkers through the machine levels to and from the elevator shafts—there would no longer be work or place for them. They would have been either completely eliminated, or assimilated into the leisure classes of the surface world of Metropolis. Either way, it would be Rotwang's revenge.

The spires of the future city are often out of focus, faraway, just as, gazing from his ocean liner, Lang saw Manhattan for the first time shimmer uncertainly before him in the twilight. These film Metropolises are frequently the domains of dictators, and we see little of the regimented life of the average citizen. Indeed, it is the architecture and the power structure of these vaster cities of tomorrow that dominate the screen. Some of the cities are on other planets—like *Flash Gordon*'s Mongo—or are even in some far future already dead and nearly vanished, like the archaeological remnants of the Krel people in *Forbidden Planet*. Whatever their designs, the street plans of these towering cities of tomorrow exist only in the cinema of the fantastic.

FREAKS

Phroso (Bozo)	Wallace Ford
Venus	Leila Hyams
Cleopatra	Olga Baclanova
Roscoe	Rosco Ates
Hercules	Henry Victor
Hans	Harry Earles
Frieda	Daisy Earles (Harry's sister)
Madame Tetrallini	Rose Dione
Siamese Twins	Daisy and Violet Hilton
Rollo Brothers	Edward Brophy, Matt McHugh
Bearded Lady	Olga Roderick
Boy with half a torso	Johnny Eck
Hindu Living Torso	Randian
Pin Heads	Schlitzie and the Snow Twins
Living Skeleton	Pete Robinson
Bird Girl	Koo Coo
Half Woman–Half Man	Josephine–Joseph
Armless Wonder	Martha Morris
Turtle Girl	Frances O'Connor
Midget	Angelo Rossito

Directed by Tod Browning
Screenplay by Willis Goldbeck and Leon Gordon
Suggested by Tod Robbins' short story "Spurs," in *Munsey's Magazine* (1923)
Dialogue by Edgar Allan Woolf and Al Boasberg
Photography: Merritt B. Gerstad
Editor: Basil Wrangell
A Dwain Esper presentation

Released by MGM February 20, 1932

Once the Cinema of the Fantastic explored a dark and frightening bypath to a sinister reality, the one reality consistent with an unreal fantasy world: a sideshow display of the ill-formed and the ugly. To take these misshapen yet human creatures and from their lives fashion a story of love and despair, of tragedy among outcasts—this was the scheme of the greatest horror director of the twenties, Tod Browning. Having proved his facility with the new sound medium by directing the immensely successful *Dracula* for Universal, Browning was in 1932 approached by MGM, for whom

in the silent days he had done many of Lon Chaney's best films, to direct a large-scale production in his specialty, the macabre. He convinced the studio that his subject should be the world of freaks—a love story and a horror story of the abnormal. He imported hundreds of sideshow and carnival performers to Hollywood from all over the world, a stream of the twisted and the grotesque. But the classic film he succeeded in making so outraged its critics and public that it was soon withdrawn by MGM and remains virtually unseen to this day. As for Browning, one of the most heralded

To the left, a bemused Tod Browning looks far milder than one would expect of the creator of the monstrous *Freaks,* a film that tells of the passion of a circus midget for a statuesque lady trapeze artist. When Hollywood's Louella Parsons, in the ad copy below, called the film "more fantastic and grotesque than any shocker," she wasn't just whistling "Dixie." *Freaks* so outraged America that it was almost immediately withdrawn; later MGM tried releasing it under a different title, *Nature's Mistakes.*

In the twilight outside the circus wagon—and in *Freaks* the shadows are often long—Hercules the strong man talks with Cleopatra the aerialist about his "rival" for her affections: the midget Hans. Later they crow over the plot they have hatched to separate the little fellow from the money he has inherited. All is not evil at the sideshow, however. In another wagon the clannish performers gather (below right) to view the bearded lady's new offspring, in a moment of joy and genuine happiness.

and innovative directors of the preceding decade, his decline was swift and certain. He was to do few other films.

Tod Browning was no stranger to dark carnival moods. He had often used characters of vaudeville and the traveling circus in previous films, always coupled with themes of evil and mystery. In *The Unholy Three* (1925) Lon Chaney, Sr., as Echo, a circus ventriloquist, and two other sideshow residents, a strong man and a midget, scheme to use their special skills against society. With Chaney masquerading as an old woman and the midget as a baby, they rob and kill.

Even more grotesque is *The Unknown,* released in 1927, its extraordinarily morbid screenplay written by Browning himself. Lon

Chaney is a circus "Armless Wonder," throwing knives and lighting matches with his agile toes. Actually, this is an acquired skill, for he has arms, hidden under a tight corset. One night, though, as he stabs the heroine's father, who opposes his suit, the girl notices the shadowy assailant has a double thumb on one hand. So Chaney decides to have his arms amputated not only to remain unsuspected of the murder, but because in a twisted rationale he also hopes it will bring him closer romantically to the heroine, who has told him she dislikes being touched! But the girl (Joan Crawford) is fickle, and, forgetting her squeamishness, falls for a muscular strong man. Enraged, Chaney plots to have his rival pulled apart by wild horses.

A contemporary critic called *The*

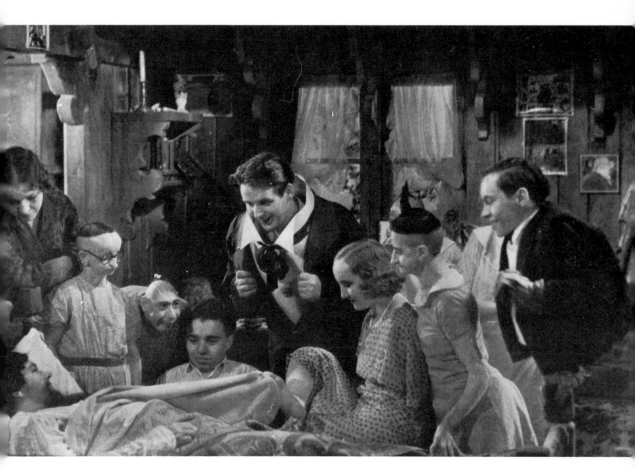

Unknown "a fiendish mingling of bloodlust, cruelty and horrors." But the Chaney film was only about a single grotesque, and an ersatz one at that. In 1932 Browning was to bring audiences into a *real* world of freaks, an incredible society where normal people were in the barely tolerated minority.

Freaks opens in the dim, dirt-caked interior of a carnival sideshow. A barker is trying to work up his small audience. "We didn't lie to you, folks. We told you we had living, breathing monstrosities! But for an accident of birth, you might be as *they* are. They did not ask to be brought into the world. Their code is a law unto themselves. Offend one—and you offend them all." The pitch holds its listeners rapt. The barker moves the crowd to a sort of open pit—for the most amazing living monstrosity of all time, he chants. We do not see what lies inside, but an onlooker screams and the crowd looks ashen. "She was once a beautiful woman," the barker shrills. "She was once known as the Peacock of the Air. . . ."

We dissolve to a circus tent interior, to Cleopatra, Queen of the Trapeze, effortlessly preening on the high wire. Below her, looking up admiringly, is the midget Hans. "She is the most beautiful *big* woman I have ever seen!" (To play these two incredible lovers, director Tod Browning chose wisely. Olga Baclanova, a famed screen siren, is Junoesque and graceful, moving like a huge, sleek, devouring animal. The midget Harry Earles, whom Browning had cast as the "baby" of *The Unholy Three* seven years earlier, was no longer young, but with his blond hair swept over his forehead he perfectly suggests boyish innocence. Betrayed and victimized as he would later be, he completely wins our empathy. From the first, we side not with our own kind, but with the freaks.)

When Hans tries to pick up Cleopatra's fallen cape, but cannot reach to place it on her shoulders, she smiles. "Are you laughing at me?" Hans asks, hurt. "Most big people do. They don't realize I'm a *man*. With the same feelings they have." Hans's sexuality established, Cleopatra gives him an encouraging pat on the cheek, and moves away smiling.

Once Browning has introduced us to the core of his drama, he widens his spectrum so that we can move further into his world of freaks. We see Madame Tetrallini, the owner of the circus, exercising a docile flock of pinheads by a forest lake. (A chance passerby is horrified; they are "horrible, twisting things, crawling and gliding," he says; but no, the good woman insists, they are like children, and God looks after them all.) But it is a rare scene that passes beyond the

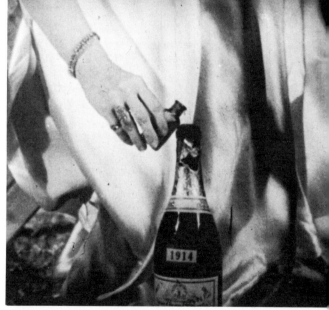

At a bizarre wedding feast, the freaks gather
to celebrate the marriage of Hans and
Cleopatra. The champagne flows. A pinhead
dances haltingly on the tabletop, and a
fire-eater performs. Cleopatra secretly empties
a phial into Hans's drink, while nearby little
Frieda, who loves Hans, sits dejectedly.

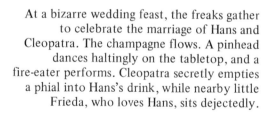

Even gentle Hans is perturbed when Cleopatra openly embraces her real lover, the strong man. Later, she teases her new husband, to the outrage of others at the wedding table. But the strange feast climaxes when the huge communal goblet of champagne is brought to her (center and below right). *"Freaks!"* she screams, and she throws the champagne at them.

circus tents. More often we are in the claustrophobic alleys behind the midway, in a vague perpetual twilight between shows, as one by one Browning lovingly unveils his collection of oddities: Josephine–Joseph, the half woman–half man, who has a sort of attraction toward Hercules, the strong man (taunts a roustabout: *"She* likes you—but *he* don't!"); Daisy and Violet, the Siamese twins, one of whom is getting married to a stammering "normal" performer the other heartily dislikes; a bearded lady who gives birth to a bearded child, whose arrival the proud father, a gangling skeleton man, celebrates by passing out cigars; Johnny, a young fellow with no lower extremities at all, moving about cheerfully and agilely on his hands.

We meet most of this strange troupe, generally happy and quite unselfconscious about themselves, as we follow about the two "normal"

The wedding feast is over. Cleopatra bears her drugged husband away in triumph while Hercules prances behind. Below left, a doctor from town expresses concern at Hans's failing health, unaware that the midget's bride has been poisoning him. Below right, a rare production portrait of director Tod Browning, standing paternally among some of the cast he assembled for *Freaks.*

lovers of the circus, a carny girl named Venus and young Bozo the clown, engagingly played by Leila Hyams and Wallace Ford. They provide a bright counterpoint to the dark theme ahead. The easy-going morality of the circus is suggested by the subtle impression that Venus has left someone else's wagon—and bed—and will soon be living with Bozo.

But dark themes *are* emerging. Cleopatra's flirtation with Hans, mere teasing at first, grows more serious as he begins showering her with gifts, and loaning her money. Talk spreads through the circus grounds. The normal workers laugh, but the freaks are apprehensive. A family of misshapen dwarfs discuss the situation: "Cleopatra isn't one of us. Why we're just filthy *things* to her. . . ." But Hans will not be stopped. He brings the buxom aerialist champagne and jewelry, while behind his back

In the darkness of night the freaks gather to strike at their enemies. Notice how the camera aims upward from near ground level as it moves with the pursuers through the mud and rain. And then the final view of Cleopatra running screaming through the trees . . . one of the most sinister moments in the cinema of the fantastic.

Cleopatra laughs at him with her real lover, the strong man Hercules. But Hercules correctly assesses one gift—a necklace—to be made of platinum and worth thousands. And Frieda, the little midget bareback rider who is in love with Hans, sobbingly pleads with Cleopatra to release Hans, accusing Cleopatra of pursuing him only because she has found out he has inherited a fortune. A fortune! Cleopatra schemes with Hercules: *"A fortune!* And I have him *like that!* I could *marry* him! Yes—he would marry me!" And, as her eyes narrow and harden as if fixing on prey, Cleopatra mutters, "Midgets are not strong . . . they could grow sick. . . ."

The next scene is subtitled "The Wedding Feast." A table has been set in the shadowy main tent of the circus, and lights strung across the top of the tent illuminate the strange festivities of the creatures assembled below. Sword-swallowers and fire-eaters perform and pinheads giggle and applaud, while Cleopatra, sitting at the head of table between Hercules and Hans, consumes glass after enormous glass of champagne, roars with drunken laughter at Hans's declarations of happiness, and openly kisses the strong

man. The freaks, responding to the flow of alcohol and no doubt to a rare celebration, work themselves into a frenzy. One by one, they begin an extraordinary chant, a singsong that makes explicit the mixed marriage they are actually toasting: "We accept her, one of us. . . ." First the dwarves. Then the bearded, the crawling, the limbless. Those who can, pound on the table with glass or knife. *"One of us, one of us . . ."* A twisted pygmy pours the contents of a champagne bottle almost as large as himself into a huge goblet and passes it to the lips of each of the wedding party. *"Gooble, gabble, one of us . . ."* The pinheads smile shyly and drink. *"One of us . . ."* The armless lady raises the goblet with her nimble toes. *"One of us . . ."* Each of the creatures drinks from the goblet, and finally it is brought to Cleopatra. But she will not take it. Repulsed by the chant, she draws herself to full height and shouts, "Freaks! *Freaks!*" She throws the contents of the goblet on the wedding party. "Now get out!" Hercules joins her in jeering at the others, now scurrying away. Only Hans remains, slumped in his chair, a broken spirit.

As the days pass, Hans grows

Mutilated and deformed by the vengeful freaks, the once arrogant Cleopatra herself becomes a sideshow attraction.

weaker—supposedly from food poisoning—and is confined to his wagon, left to the attentions of his new bride. She is kind and loving—and careful to see he takes his medicine. Always, though, there is a face at the window observing her every move. Whenever she leaves the wagon, there is a shuffling almost underfoot, as an advance guard of the circus creatures hurries away into the darkness. Even Hans no longer accepts her medicine, but secretly spits it away: "I will never forget what you are doing to me, Cleo." When the amazon finds an excuse to visit the strong man, Hans smiles mischievously. He whispers to a friend, as small as himself—we, the audience, are now on their level, for the camera has made Cleopatra grotesque and out-of-frame—*"Tonight!"*

It is a grim night. Lightning flashes stab the darkness, and thunder rolls nearby. The first sight we have of the night is from a vantage point *beneath the wagon wheels,* as we follow the legless Johnny hopping on his hands from shelter to shelter. Soon the wagons begin to move through the rain and the mud: the circus is pulling stakes for another town. Inside Hans's trailer, Cleo is just about to give the midget his medicine, when Hans insists upon seeing the bottle from which she has poured it. She is shocked. Hans is sitting up, and behind him are several of his friends, menacing her with a knife or a pistol or a stick. She screams and backs away, as the wagon hits a tree in the rain and collapses. Hercules comes to her rescue, and the small people inside are no match for the brutish strong man. Even Bozo, the clown, who tries to rescue Hans by taking on Hercules, is no match. The strong man beats him to the floor and steps outside the wagon into the storm, looking for Cleo, who has by this time fled.

As his eyes grow accustomed to the lightning-streaked darkness, he sees a blood-curdling sight. Stretched out before him, in the rain and the mud, are all the misshapen freaks of the carnival. Broken bodies, limbless bodies, twisted bodies, each with a knife, and each *crawling toward him!* With a moan, Hercules turns away, but he slips in the mud and cannot get far. The creatures wriggle steadily foward, like an unstoppable army of large dark insects, knives clenched in teeth or toes or flippers, determined to reach their prey. And what will they do when they have caught him? . . . Emasculation? A quick death from rapid stabbings? We do not know, for the action shifts to Cleopatra, running screaming through a dark wood. Behind her in the forest scurries a pack of creatures—moving surely, swiftly, even joyously— illuminated briefly in a single lightning flash. We hear Cleopatra scream once more, and then there is only darkness and silence.

We switch back to the sideshow setting on which *Freaks* opened. The barker, standing over the intriguing pit, is finishing his story: "How she got that way will never be known. Some say a jealous lover. Others . . . the code of the freaks. . . ."

And we look down upon what was once Cleopatra, now a crouched figure on a bed of straw, a figure that looks incredibly like a huge woman-chicken: tufted, flappered, lame, scarred, half-blind, mindless, and clucking. Bent over, she is now only as tall as Hans, and far more macabre an oddity than he: she is completely subhuman.

Tod Browning expected *Freaks* to be dynamic enough to stun the critics; the film did more than that. Reaction to it was swift and terrible. Newspapers denounced it, PTA groups rallied against it, and theater managers refused to play it. A leading trade journal declared the film as "so loathsome that

I am nauseated thinking about it. The producers give an excuse that these creatures are all in the circus, implying that the characterizations are not out of keeping with the conditions that may be imagined as existing in a circus. But this does not give them the right to do with them what the picture does. It is not fit to be shown anywhere."

MGM, in a desperate attempt to soften the shock of the film, spliced a long cautionary preface to it, a printed warning that carefully explained—under the heading "Special Message"—that "history and religion, folklore and legend abound in tales of misshapen misfits who have altered the world's course. Goliath, Caliban, Frankenstein, Gloucester, Tom Thumb, and Kaiser Wilhelm, are just a few. . . ." After lavishing some paragraphs on how freaks were social outcasts in past ages, the preface hastens to assure us that "the majority of freaks are endowed with normal thoughts and emotions." Happily, "never again will such a story be filmed, as modern science and teratology is rapidly eliminating such blunders of nature from the world."

But this cautionary whitewash did nothing to stem the adverse tide of reaction to the film. Ultimately MGM felt forced to withdraw the film from circulation. In nearly forty years, its screenings have been few.

Tod Browning's career also was close to its finish. Three years later he attempted to remake of one of his greatest silent successes, *London After Midnight* (1927), which had starred the now-dead Lon Chaney. The remake, called *The Mark of the Vampire* (1935), had vampires floating about a haunted house, but explained them rationally at the end in detective-story fashion, counter to the mood of the film. It was a box-office failure. The following year's film, *The Devil Doll,* was slightly better, particularly due to its clever special effects—it had miniature people (not midgets, but inch-high beings reduced to that size by evil science) committing murders as acts of vengeance for Lionel Barrymore, who has escaped from Devil's Island and has avoided capture by dressing as a woman. Even this, however, was not enough to renew Browning's career. The year 1939 saw the release of *Miracles for Sale,* a mystery set among stage magicians, a group of people much like carnival performers, but this was his last directorial effort. He retired, his pure love for the screen grotesque and fantastic uncompromised, to a large castlelike California home and died at the age of eighty, thirty years after his defeat at the hands of *Freaks.*

KING KONG

Ann Darrow	Fay Wray
Carl Denham	Robert Armstrong
Jack Driscoll	Bruce Cabot
Englehorn	Frank Reicher
Weston	Sam Hardy
Native Chief	Noble Johnson
Second Mate	James Flavin
Witch King	Steve Clemento
Charlie (Cook)	Victor Wong
and	

King Kong, the Eighth Wonder of the World!

Directed by Merian C. Cooper and Ernest B. Schoedsack
Screenplay by James Creelman and Ruth Rose
Story by Edgar Wallace and Merian C. Cooper
Technical director: Willis O'Brien
Director of Photography: Edward Linden
Music: Max Steiner
Editor: Ted Cheesman
Executive Producer: David O. Selznick

Released by RKO Pictures April 7, 1933

He was a king in the world he knew—and a monarch in our world as well. RKO's billing of him as "the eighth wonder" may have been several shades too modest, for Kong's fame has endured, undiminished, through nearly four decades. The popularity of the incredible *King Kong* has not slackened since its release in 1933; new generations in countries across the world continue to thrill to the hopeless love the great ape offers the blonde, and to the heartrending story of how this love drives him from his jungle fastness to destruction in the metropolis.

The kinship between ape and man has fascinated us ever since Darwin called them cousins; tales of possible unions between the two have had a certain pulp popularity, more as subtle folk anagrams of sexual and racial fears. But *Kong* transcends all the gorilla plays that preceded it in the twenties and early thirties, for it is finer, nobler, and made of different stuff: the ingredient is love. We are meant to love Kong. Unique among cinema apes (Lon Chaney, Sr. ape-men, Edgar Allen Poe ape-murderers, and many others from a more turbulent day of screen melodrama), Kong alone was not designed to disgust, rape, or kill. He did not track helpless victims or train to dispense a human master's private vengeance. And although Kong's pursuit through the film of a doll-sized human female has the makings on several levels of a perverse erotic fantasy, we know such is not the case: Kong's motives are pure. And his death is not a triumphant climax, but a tragedy.

This unparalleled romantic adventure was made with such imagination that its virtues seem to become stronger and more apparent with each passing year. And yet it is inseparable from the decade of its origin, the Depression thirties, from which it draws its innocence, its helplessness, its honest passion and earnest heroism. To call *King Kong* a great fantasy film is to measure it by too short a yardstick. It is above every category, simply a great film.

It is difficult to believe that *Kong* was planned at first as a semidocumentary travelogue. The guiding genius behind its creation,

Merian C. Cooper, was an adventurer, explorer, and newspaperman who entered show business by producing, with a cameraman friend named Ernest B. Schoedsack and a woman foreign correspondent, Marguerite Harrison, an incredible film document called *Grass,* a record of their expedition to Persia to follow the migration of a primitive tribe in search of grazing land. The film was designed for the lecture circuit, but a Paramount executive happened to see it and put it into theatrical release. It made money, and its unabashed excitement—Cooper was after all a writer and a romantic, and his document was not flat film but full of zesty life, bursting with human adventure in a far reach of the world—won warm praise from the critics. Cooper and Schoedsack decided their next adventure would be film-making.

Chang, released two years after *Grass* in 1927, was both a jungle documentary (the locale is Siam) and a nonstop thriller. Carefully constructing their basic story line in advance—a pioneering family carving a home in a wilderness—and splicing to it every last bit of excitement they could find in two years spent on location, Cooper and Schoedsack achieved the prototype and inspiration of all future travelogue features. A reviewer of the day hailed *Chang* as "the most remarkable film of wild beast life that has reached the screen. . . . Man-eating tigers, furious elephants in thundering stampedes, leopards, bears, monkeys, snakes and other animals are shown in . . . one tense thrill after another."

At the New York premiere its innovative producers enhanced the eye-popping visual effects of the film by suddenly enlarging the screen —through a device they called the "magnoscope" (a specially installed projector lens and screen framing device)—to three-times its normal size

50

as when the *changs* (a native word for elephants) rush into and destroy a village, or when a maddened tiger leaps up at a treed hunter. (This memorable shot was achieved by Schoedsack from above, his camera just inches from the animal's teeth.) The quick widening of the screen at these feverish moments had the effect of suddenly plunging audiences into the churning action: it was a powerful cinematic device, but only secondary to the brilliance of a cinematic documentary whose carefully structured thrills set the pace for all jungle travelogues and jungle adventure films to come.

In the next few years Cooper and Schoedsack attempted to adjust their own special talents to the mainstream of motion pictures; they were hired to provide African location footage for possible use in a production of *The Four Feathers* (1929); and Indian sequences were shot but scarcely used years later, in 1935, for Gary Cooper's *Lives of a Bengal Lancer.* At this time the shrewdly progressive Merian Cooper invested heavily in airplane stock and became one of the first leaders of that rapidly expanding industry. However, his inquiring mind had been intrigued by the monkeys and baboons with which he had worked extensively in both *Chang* and *The Four Feathers.* Their very human postures had given him the germ of an idea for a new film. It was not a very hard idea to come by, as the previous decade had certainly been the decade of the great ape: Darwin debated at street corners and in court, and the relationships and similarities of gorilla and man everywhere discussed. What, Cooper thought, if a huge gorilla were suddenly lured—by a woman? by love?—into the world of men, into the metropolis, and then destroyed?

Cooper's initial conception involved the use of an actual gorilla, made larger by trick photography, in actual African settings. He would call the film—he had a fondness for short, dynamic-sounding titles—*Kong. King Kong.* He took the idea to David Selznick, then in New York to raise money for some film projects planned with his brother Myron. Selznick was impressed with the idea and with Cooper, and when he was put in charge of production at RKO the following year (1931), he called in Cooper to help him. Eventually Cooper was made his executive assistant. As Selznick's aide, his work included reviewing possible studio projects. One such was a proposed film about animal life at the dawn of time, called *Creation.* After one look at animator Willis O'Brien's test sequences of dinosaurs in a prehistoric landscape, Cooper abandoned the idea of filming *Kong* on safari in the uncertain jungles, abandoned the idea of using an actual gorilla at all. He would create *Kong* in the RKO studio—and eventually he used for his giant ape a steel-skeletoned doll only eighteen inches high!

The genius of Willis O'Brien had already been demonstrated in *The Lost World.* But his contribution to *Kong* can hardly be overestimated. The painstaking stop-motion camera process by which rigid figures on a landscape—O'Brien's favorite work area was a tabletop layout in the garage behind his house—were frame-photographed, moved slightly, and frame-photographed again, until the effect of living, breathing movement was achieved, seemed an unlikely source of a creature so individualized that he came to be loved by millions. Yet this is what the great O'Brien achieved. His bag of tricks was full (rear projection, the projection of humans on a tiny screen set up within a miniature set, all the resources of matting) and he worked in secret; few knew or, knowing, would believe that the towering Kong was actually a

puppet scarcely bigger than a rule. For
years after the film's release a folk
legend persisted that the creature was a
big motorized robot with several men
inside; actually, a full-scale head had
been built, and an arm and foot. The
head was constructed with gnashing
teeth principally to photograph Kong
chewing on a live native. The giant foot
was built solely to descend upon
terrified natives, grinding them into the
earth. Both these scenes were
ultimately deleted from the film. But
the enormous arm and hand are often
seen, nearly always tenderly clutching
the heroine. Frequently the full-scale
arm with human being in tow is matted
up against Kong's tiny animated puppet
body, making an ingenious and unusual
process shot: the inches-high gorilla
looking down at his ten-foot-long arm!
Of course, looking is what Kong—or
should we say O'Brien?—did best: his
quizzical, bewildered, very human
expressions are unforgettable.

Meanwhile Merian Cooper was filling
in the details of his fantastic plot: from
the beginning he had envisioned Kong
amok in the great city of New York,
ultimately meeting his match and his
end atop the recently completed
concrete colossus, the Empire State
Building. (An alternate, discarded finish
was to have Kong trapped and shot
down inside Yankee Stadium.) The
famed English mystery writer Edgar
Wallace, under contract to RKO,
worked on the story with Cooper, and
either deliberately or unconsciously
much of the structure of *The Lost
World* was borrowed: a giant
prehistoric creature is discovered in a
remote, unexplored part of the world;
the creature is brought to civilization,
breaks free, and is killed. (Of course the
ingredient that the Conan Doyle
precursor omitted was the love affair at
the core of *Kong.*) When Wallace died
of a heart attack, complicated by
pneumonia, much of his contribution

52

The celebrated mystery writer Edgar Wallace,
pipe-dreaming about the Kong he helped
create. He did not live to enjoy the incredible
popularity of this gigantic jungle beast who
was to conquer the hearts of the world,
winning an affection that shows no signs of
abating.

Weak, starving, Ann Darrow allows herself to be rescued by fast-talking producer Carl Denham.

was reshaped, with a good deal of the final dialogue written by Ernest Schoedsack's wife, Ruth Rose, a former actress and explorer who later had some success as a screenwriter. Among othe things, she wrote the script for *The Last Days of Pompeii* (1935) and Cooper's version of *She* (also 1935).

Cooper chose his cast with care from players available to RKO. Bruce Cabot and Robert Armstrong were leading men who had already done several pictures for the studio. For his heroine Cooper selected Fay Wray, who had demonstrated her aptitude for thrillers in *Mystery of the Wax Museum* (1933) and Cooper's own *The Most Dangerous Game,* made literally at the same time as *Kong* but released a year earlier because of *Kong*'s time-consuming

animation work. Because the same studio jungle was used for both films, Fay Wray often had to plunge terrified through the same underbrush twice over! Her grace, her honest beauty, her screams—especially her screams— catapulted her amongst the immortals. Her identification with *King Kong* is so complete that it blots out any other vestige of her career from memory and even, I suspect, from the public records. She is Kong's girl, beyond question. Like the sacrificial offering Kong took her to be, Fay Wray surrendered herself to this one-in-a-lifetime part; even though she played character roles as late as the mid-1950s and accepts an occasional interview to this day, *King Kong* eclipses all. She is the perfect heroine: love-object, femme fatale,

Denham coaches Ann in a shipboard screen test—"Scream! Scream as if you meant it!"

American beauty. The beauty that killed the beast.

The score to *King Kong* was composed by RKO's resident musical director Max Steiner, who in the last few years had written scores for, among other films, *Cimarron* (1931) and *A Bill of Divorcement* (1932). His rich and *agitato* music always complemented melodrama and adventure films, but for *Kong* he soared above anything he had done previously. No doubt caught by the nobility of the film's theme, Steiner translated it into a musical dimension that perfectly underscored the story's terror and pathos. From the moment the words *King Kong* appear starkly on the screen and the credits unreel, the Max Steiner music stirs the audience with a lush crescendo that carefully

builds up and up. It is a masterpiece.

Cooper, a master showman, spent months on a tease publicity campaign (actually similar to the one launched within the film by the Robert Armstrong character) that was purposely vague as to who or what Kong actually was. In movie-house "coming attractions" a shadow crossing the screen was used to herald the "coming of Kong"—with no further explanation offered. The film was premiered at dual openings in New York, at both the gilded Roxy and the newly opened cinema showcase, the Radio City Music Hall. Kong himself, billed as "the eighth wonder of the world," is the last name in the credits, followed by "An Old Arab Proverb" to set the mood for what is to follow:

55

And the prophet said: And lo, the beast looked upon the face of beauty. And it stayed its hand from killing. And from that day, it was as one dead.

King Kong opens at the New York docks at night. Sailors and dock workers alike have been whispering about the mystery ship chartered by theatrical producer Carl Denham; he is described in words that might have fitted as well *Kong*'s co-director Ernest Schoedsack: "They say he ain't scared of nothing. If he wants a picture of a lion he just goes up to him and tells him to look pleasant." On board there is more crew than generally carried, enough explosives to blow up the harbor, and gas bombs that could stun elephants. One thing Denham has not been able to supply is a girl to play heroine for a film odyssey he is planning into uncharted wilds; he has the reputation of being too reckless. "Nonsense," snorts the producer, "there are girls in more danger in this city tonight than they ever would be with *me*." The ship must leave by the morning tide; Denham decides he will

The reefs of Skull Island, over which a great wall towers. What does it hold back? Carl Denham and his movie company have a closer look and encounter a native tribe.

find a girl that night in the New York streets.

Many hours later a dejected Denham is about to give up when he chances to see a girl, obviously hungry, reach haltingly for an apple from a sidewalk fruit stand. The proprietor pops out and accuses the girl of trying to steal, but she has done no such thing, and Denham pays for the fruit. The girl nearly faints in his arms; she is half-starved, weak, and very, very beautiful. Carl Denham has found his heroine.

Later, Carl feeds the girl in a diner. She is Ann Darrow, a typical Depression girl on her own; she has no family and has just had a run of bad luck. She has done some acting as an extra at studios on Long Island, now closed. She is exactly what Denham has been searching for. "I've got a job for you—money, adventure, and fame, the thrill of a lifetime . . . and a long sea voyage that starts at six o'clock tomorrow morning." Ann hesitates, and Denham assures her he is on the level. "Trust me, and keep your chin up."

The tramp ship begins its journey to a destination somewhere west of Sumatra, in completely uncharted waters. For Ann it is a relaxed and happy time, even though tough first mate Jack Driscoll is somewhat unsettled at having a woman aboard and lets her know it. The crew is restless in the extreme, for no one

knows where the ship is really heading. One day, far into the Pacific, Denham reveals to the ship's captain and Jack Driscoll their port of call: a small island not on any map. He had heard of it from the skipper of a Norwegian bark, who in turn learned of it from a dying native whose canoe had blown far out to sea. The island has a shoreline that is nearly all sheer cliff, hundreds of feet high, and across the narrowest part of the island runs a high, thick wall, built uncounted centuries ago. The natives living on the island now keep the wall in constant repair . . . as if *keeping something out.* "Did you ever hear of Kong?" Denham asks. Captain Englehorn has heard the word and thinks it refers to some sort of native god or spirit. "Neither beast nor man," replies Denham. "Something monstrous, all-powerful, still living . . . holding that island in a grip of fear."

Days later, trapped in a thick fog, they hear native drumbeats in the distance. They are close to their destination: an island easily recognizable by a mountain shaped like a skull. The next morning the fog lifts, and Skull Island is before them, with its wall—which looks possibly Egyptian in origin—plainly seen cutting across the green jungles. Denham organizes a landing party, including Ann, for he's learned long ago always to have his cast and cameras ready when scouting new locations.

A fantastic sight greets them: a band of natives dancing ritualistically before the wall, moaning *"Kong! Kong!"* They easily spot the chief of the tribe and, next to him, a scared native girl,

At night black shapes pull Ann from the ship. On the island, the natives strap her to an altar at the wall's gates, as if she were an offering of some kind. Frenzied, they appear to be awaiting some one . . . some thing. . . .

covered with flower garlands. Is she to be in some way a sacrifice? Denham starts to film the weird ceremony, and he and his men are discovered. The natives are plainly unsettled at being interrupted, but Denham—through Captain Englehorn, who knows most of the Malay dialects—tries to make friendly gestures. The chief suddenly sees Ann—and offers six of his wives in trade for the blonde. She has obviously made an impression, for the native chief moves forward menacingly. Denham hastily turns down his offer and waves good-bye until tomorrow; the landing party about-faces for a quick retreat.

That night a native canoe moves silently toward the freighter anchored offshore. Ann is on deck alone. Dark hands in war paint reach for her. Before she can scream, she is snatched from the ship.

Ann's absence is soon noticed by Jack Driscoll—already in love with the girl—who curses Denham for exposing her to danger. From the deck they see the native village ablaze with light; another ceremony is in progress. A rescue party, armed with guns, sets out at once.

But beside the great wall Ann is in serious trouble. Natives have dragged her to a high altar behind giant gates set in the wall and have strapped each of her arms to a stone column. Struggling to free herself from between the twin columns, Ann watches in terror as the natives retreat, closing and bolting the giant gates behind them! Then she sees they are lined along the top of the wall, waiting, as she is waiting . . . but for what

A party from the ship, penetrating deep into the island's jungles in an effort to rescue Ann, finds itself in a dangerous prehistoric world.

From deep in the jungle in front of Ann comes a horrifying roar, and the sound of trees trampled and uprooted. Ann begins to scream. And then she sees *Kong* . . . an incredible hulking beast, a giant gorilla more than thirty feet high, *moving toward her.* Strangely, despite his roars, he shows more curiosity than menace. Certainly she is the first blonde he has ever seen. He picks her from the altar with his giant paw, and they disappear together into the darkness.

Denham and Driscoll have seen all this and, with a rescue party, manage to open the gates and move into the world beyond the wall. It is an incredible world full of prehistoric beasts, and they are almost immediately attacked by and forced to shoot a stegosaurus, with mean eyes and armor-plated hide.

Their attempt to ford a steamy swamp with a quickly made raft is far less fortunate: as they drift across the fog-shrouded water, what looks at first like a sea serpent rears its head. It is actually a plesiosaurus, and with its terrible, huge mouth it picks up three of the crew and kills them before the men can scramble to the safety of the shore.

In complete panic, the crew members rush deeper into the jungle and attempt to cross a fallen tree trunk bridging a ravine. Suddenly Kong appears at the other side, without Ann (he has placed her high in the branches of another tree nearby), and the hulking creature loosens the trunk and sends it hurtling—with the humans still clinging to it—hundreds of feet down to the rocks below. (Cooper and O'Brien

A crew member tries in vain to escape deadly jaws. On page following, from the hollow of another tree Kong scoops up his diminutive prize.

had originally planned to animate giant spiders at the bottom of the ravine in this sequence, but the idea was abandoned.) Jack Driscoll, who had not yet reached the trunk when Kong attacked, hides in a cave by the ravine's edge; he appears to be the only member of his group still alive.

Ann's screams from her treetop perch brings Kong scurrying back. A great Tyrannosaurus rex, his massive, leering mouth filled with a hundred teeth, has found the girl and is moving toward her on powerful hind legs. Kong intercepts the carnivorous monster, and there is a fierce struggle, with both creatures thrashing through the jungle below a terrified Ann. Finally Kong snaps his opponent's neck and beats his own chest in a roar of victory. Picking Ann up once more, the giant ape continues his lumbering trek through the wilderness. Jack manages to follow. On the way he runs into Carl Denham, the only other survivor of the entire rescue party. In a hurried, whispered conference they agree that Jack should continue tracking Kong and the girl, while Denham will go back for help and gas bombs. They separate.

Kong's home is a vast cliffside cave. It is dark and dank, and volcanic vapors float toward the stalactites. Here he places Ann tenderly upon a ledge—and almost immediately must fight a giant snake slithering up toward her. Then he brings his newfound blond toy out on a cliff terrace and starts to play with it. (When Kong first carried his human captive into the jungle depths, there was a sequence where he fondled her with his forefinger, removed her dress out of sheer curiosity, and then sniffed at the clothes in puzzled wonder. Ann is so small in his paw the scene is completely unoffending, yet it was removed from all but the first release prints.)

Kong puts Ann down for a moment—and a great pterodactyl,

63

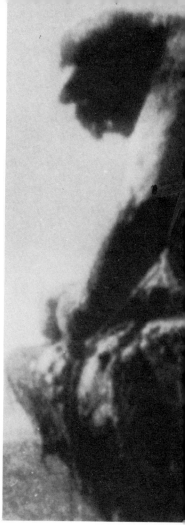

wings flapping, swoops down and snatches the girl in its claws. Kong reaches up to save her, and a wild struggle begins. Ann has been dropped by the prehistoric flying reptile, and she cowers behind some rocks. Suddenly she sees Jack! He motions her silently to the edge of the cliff, and they climb hand over hand down some vines into the sea. Kong, after pounding his enemy to death, spots their escape and tries to stop it. But he is too late.

Kong is not to be denied so easily, however. Jack and Ann make it to the safety of the wall, but Denham, waiting by its gates, knows that Kong will not be far behind. He is right; the whole jungle trembles as if to thunder, and the beast's great fists hammer at the entranceway. The entire native population pressed against the other side of the wall cannot contain him, and the gates burst open. The giant Kong runs amok through the village. (In the original release Kong popped helpless natives into his mouth and chewed them, grinding other natives into the ground with his heel; in the 1938 reissue of the film these shots were deleted to suit the sensibilities of

Kong almost loses his prize to the claws of a great pterodactyl, but fights off the winged creature. He is not so successful with Jack Driscoll. The heroic seaman escapes with Ann by climbing down some vines that hang from Kong's high cliff home. Kong is furious as they drop into the sea.

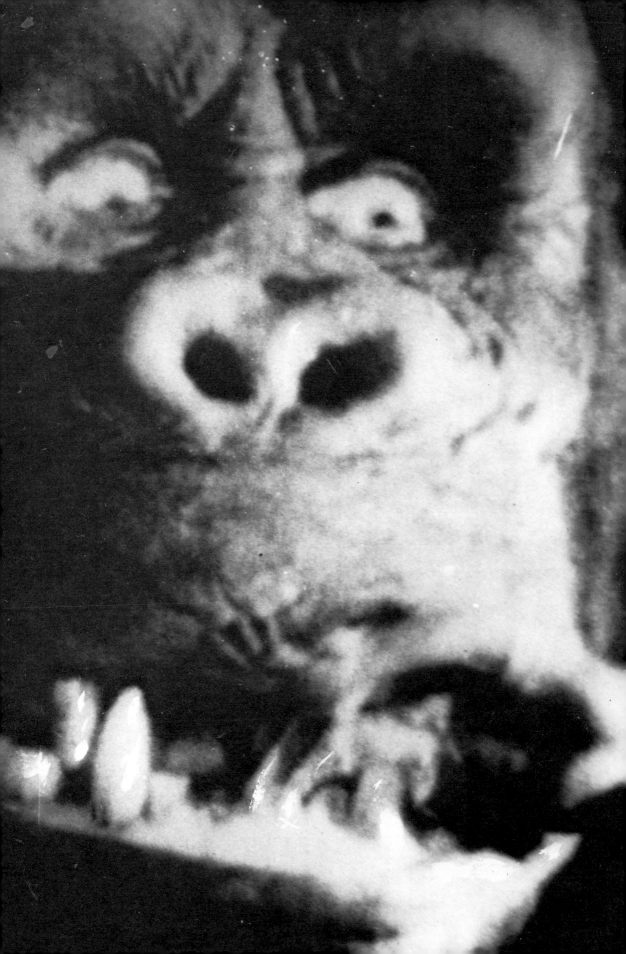

the new strict Production Code. As well, all scenes of Kong in violent action were deliberately toned darker, so his frenzy would be less perceivable and therefore have less impact.) After some carnage, Denham manages to explode his gas bombs. The great beast is felled. Denham immediately sees the immense exhibition possibilities of his prize. "We're millionaires, boys!" He will bring Kong himself back to civilization.

It is New York, some months later. A first-night audience is crowding into a Broadway theater, puzzled over Carl Denham's mysterious new offering, wondering who or what King Kong—identified on the marquee only as "the eighth wonder of the world"—actually is. Backstage, Ann is nervous and Jack Driscoll, uncomfortable but dashing in evening clothes, is concerned for her. The suave, confident Carl Denham steps before the curtains and addresses his audience. "I'm going to show you the

Two scenes that for years have not been seen in *King Kong* prints: the great beast chewing on a native and crushing another underfoot.

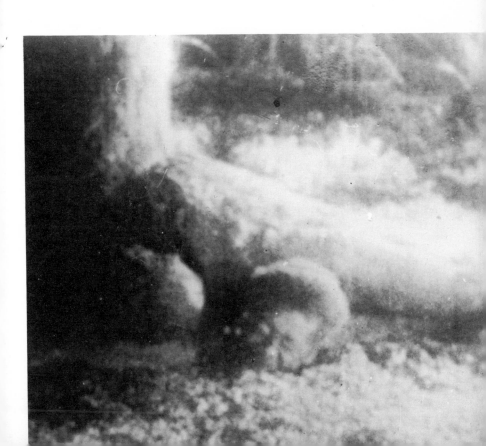

greatest thing your eyes have ever beheld. He was a king and a god in the world he knew, but now he comes to civilization merely a captive, a show to gratify your curiosity. Ladies and gentlemen, *look at KONG!*" The curtain lifts. The audience is stunned. There stands Kong, in massive chains, a great steel halter about his neck. Denham continues smoothly, introducing Ann, "the bravest girl I've ever known. There the beast—here the beauty." Denham then invites Driscoll onstage, with "the gentlemen of the press, so that you can watch them take the first pictures of Kong in captivity." Flashbulbs begin popping. A great many of them. The giant beast begins to pull at his chains; he thinks the reporters are trying to harm the girl. Suddenly he pulls free; the theater is in pandemonium as he bursts his way through the back wall and onto the street. In the meantime Jack has pulled Ann to safety through the stampeding audience and up to her room in a nearby hotel, not knowing that Kong has sensed she is somewhere inside the

Kong in New York. Below, his theatrical debut. Opposite, Kong, now escaped, searches for—and finds—his beloved Ann, hiding in a nearby hotel room.

Planes search out the fugitive Kong, who has taken refuge atop the city's highest point: the spire of the Empire State Building. It provides no sanctuary from the bullets of the air squadron, and, riddled, the great beast falls to his death.

building and is slowly climbing the outside wall. Ann shrieks with terror as first the great eye peers through the window, and a giant paw inexorably draws her, bed and all, to the beast clutching the wall outside, high above the crowds pointing to Kong's dangerous perch! (In the original release of the film, Kong in his climb up the building grabs another girl by mistake and, realizing his error, casually tosses her away—down hundreds of feet to the street below.) Clutching his prize tightly, he swings from building to building, momentarily placing Ann on a rooftop so that he can do battle with a train careening along the old Sixth Avenue El. Seeing the great beast ripping his way through the elevated tracks, the motorman of the oncoming

Kong topples from his high perch, and Ann, whom he has carried with him to the top of the Empire State Building, is rescued. A love story has come to a tragic end: "It was beauty killed the beast."

train comes to a emergency stop—and Kong seizes the first car and its startled contents, derails it, and hurls it to the street below, battering it and the doomed passengers inside with his giant fists. Then, reclaiming Ann, he begins his journey of destruction through the metropolis. "Attention, all stations," the police radio blares, "Kong is heading for the Empire State Building." At police headquarters, a worried Carl Denham and Jack Driscoll discuss the dim possibility of rescuing Ann. "Airplanes," Jack suddenly shouts, brightening. "If he should put Ann down, and the planes could get close enough to pick him off . . ."

Kong has reached the Empire State Building; for him it represents the safety of the highest tree. He starts to climb—up and up the almost sheer side of this fantastic modern building, constructed only a few short years before. He makes it to the very top and tenderly deposits Ann on the highest ledge. Suddenly he hears the drone of the plane motors; six small army fighters dart into view, and the great ape roars his defiance. The lead plane breaks formation and dives at him, machine guns chattering. Kong feels pain. More and more of the metal birds swoop down at him, menacing him; the beast manages to grab the wingtip of one to send it hurtling into the side of the building, then down in flames to the street. But the others keep strafing him. Kong is bleeding from chest and neck; he is weakening, dizzy, unable to hang onto his spire. He picks Ann up for one last sad look of love and places her back on her perch. As soon as he does so, the planes move in for the kill. The great shaggy monarch of beasts, trapped here in an alien world, clutches at his throat, totters backward—and falls.

For Ann, it is rescue and safety. Jack Driscoll climbs up from the observatory platform and holds her in his arms. Far below, the body of Kong fills a city street, with police and barricades keeping back a milling, curious crowd. A bemused Carl Denham, still in evening clothes, pushes through and is allowed to examine the massive corpse, his now-dead eighth wonder. "Well, Denham, the airplanes got him," says a police official in triumph. The producer shakes his head wryly and speaks among the most famous last words of any film: *"Oh, no—it wasn't the airplanes. It was beauty killed the beast."*

King Kong was an instant smash and has remained so. Even television has not sapped its vigor; indeed, it has been one of the medium's greatest audience-getters. And rightly so; *Kong* is an authentic masterpiece and has all the appeal and reach one would expect from a great work of art.

But duplicating a work of art is a difficult process. Less than a year later Cooper and O'Brien (with Schoedsack directing, from a story by Ruth Rose) brought out *Son of Kong,* an offspring hard to explain, as the father was supposedly millions of years old and unmated. In the film Denham returns to Skull Island to discover both a playful, albino "baby Kong" and a secret diamond treasure—the latter very providentially, as seemingly half of New York City has sued him for the havoc caused by Kong Senior. At the film's end an earthquake causes Skull Island to sink, and the noble, self-sacrificing white gorilla holds Denham, his party, and the treasure in the hollow of his great paw until a boat can rescue them—and then he drowns. Sensing that the follow-up was made quickly to cash in on the original *Kong,* audiences reacted badly to the film, and it has been rather unfairly forgotten.

Willis O'Brien continued to work on many of Merian Cooper's productions:

73

among them, the fantastic scenes of destruction in the closing reels of *The Last Days of Pompeii* (1935). He was not to come into his own again, however, until the release of *Mighty Joe Young* (1949) sixteen years later. In many ways *Young* paralleled *King Kong,* but Cooper lessened its impact by reducing this new giant gorilla's savageness, unwisely making the film more of a children's fairy story than, as *Kong* has been, a love story for all ages. Terry Moore is an African ranch owner's daughter who has raised a massive black gorilla, which she calls Joe Young, from infancy; a traveling rodeo headed by (naturally) showman Robert Armstrong chances upon the beast, and he persuades Terry that both she and her pet belong in a Broadway nightclub. Their personal appearances—the girl sings "Beautiful Dreamer" at a piano held aloft by Young—are cut short when a drunk patron causes the gorilla to run amok, spectacularly smashing the club, with its African veldt motif and glass-caged lions, to splintered ruin. Happily, however, Young's life is spared, for as he is about to be mowed down by the police he rescues some children trapped in a burning orphanage. His show-business career over, Joe Young quietly lives out his life back at the African ranch, the first movie monster to make it alive and well beyond the closing credits. He had very little of the menace of his predecessor and certainly nothing of Kong's romantic soul, but he earned a good deal of money and won for Willis O'Brien a much-deserved Academy Award.

Although Willis O'Brien contributed much to such films as *The Animal World* (1956) and *The Giant Behemoth* (1959), his career beyond his association with Cooper seems to have been largely spent creating great ideas that no one had the foresight to let him film. He died in 1962, leaving behind many frustrated projects and unfinished dreams. Happily, his inspiration to such new animators as Ray Harryhausen and Jim Danforth continues the screen magic he pioneered. He fathered a very special art, and the definitive assessment of his genius has yet to be made.

Merian Cooper is still in the midst of a very successful career. Before leaving RKO in 1949, he produced some of the screen's greatest Westerns in association with John Ford, and later he brought a new dimension to the travel film with the Cinerama process he helped to pioneer. Always an explorer of new vistas and new techniques, Cooper is very reminiscent of Carl Denham—the adventurer and the showman united in one. The Denham who moves through the jungle brush of Skull Island is very much the Cooper of *Grass* and *Chang,* risking everything in a dangerous setting far from civilization. One would like to think that there, on some troubled trek, perhaps deep in some uncharted jungle terrain, his path crossed that of the creature who inspired his Kong. Cooper has much else of which to be proud—*Stagecoach* (1939) and *The Quiet Man* (1952) were his projects, for example—but his *King Kong* climbed the very pinnacle of the fantastic cinema.

THE BLACK CAT

Hjalmar Poelzig	Boris Karloff
Dr. Vitus Werdegast	Bela Lugosi
Peter Alison	David Manners
Joan Alison	Jacqueline Wells (Julie Bishop)
Majordomo	Egon Brecher
Thamal	Harry Cording
The Maid	Ann Duncan
Karen Werdegast/Karen Poelzig	Lucille Lund
Sergeant	Henry Armetta
Lieutenant	Albert Conti
Cultists	Peggy Terry
	King Baggott
	Lois January
	Symona Boniface
	Virginia Ainsworth
	Michael Mark
	John Carradine (organist)

Directed by Edgar G. Ulmer
Screenplay by Peter Ruric
Story by Edgar G. Ulmer and Peter Ruric
Suggested by the story by Edgar Allan Poe
Music: Heinz Roemheld
Photography: John Mescall
Editor: Ray Curtiss
Art Director: Charles D. Hall

Released by Universal May 7, 1934

The Black Cat deals with the struggle between good and evil science, personified above by Bela Lugosi (left) and Boris Karloff. Each face betrays a tortured spirit, well caught in this landmark film of the dark fantastic by director Edgar G. Ulmer, shown, seated in the foreground, in a pensive moment in this rare production still.

By 1934 the founder and very Teutonic head of Universal Pictures, "Uncle Carl" Laemmle (who was called that not only because of his paternalistic ways but because many of his family had jobs at the studio), had fully realized that the horror film market was providing his studio with a good deal of its revenue. This market Universal had itself created with the release of Bela Lugosi in *Dracula* in the early part of 1931 and Boris Karloff in *Frankenstein* some months thereafter. Each player had made considerable

impact in his role; why not combine both in a single film? And furthermore, why not endow this film with a high order of horror "class" by drawing it from the works of Edgar Allan Poe, specifically, the story of "The Black Cat"?

Poe had not been neglected by the early film-makers. D. W. Griffith, in particular, used Poe's life and works as the basis for several films in the silent era. Just the year before Universal went into production of *The Black Cat*, a German film called *Terrible Stories*

(Unheimliche Geschichte)—three interconnecting episodes in the capture of a madman—used the same Poe story for the first of the episodes, sticking fairly closely to the account of a wife-murderer who inadvertently seals a cat in the alcove into which he bricks up his wife's body: the animal's cries betray him to the police and disorder his mind.

Laemmle was very aware of production work in Europe; indeed he hired a European-trained young Austrian, Edgar G. Ulmer, then only thirty, as director, to ensure that his film would have the proper Germanic Gothic atmosphere. Ulmer, who had assisted the great German director of *Nosferatu* and *Faust,* F. W. Murnau, succeeded only too well. The story, from a treatment by Ulmer and Peter Ruric, and merely "based on the immortal Edgar Allan Poe classic," made only incidental use of the black cat theme, dismissing Poe almost entirely, for a completely original story of devil worship and black mass orgies in the Balkans.

And yet, even though violating the letter and the spirit of Poe, *The Black Cat* is a fascinating dark landmark in the cinema of the fantastic. Never were the rituals of witchcraft more completely presented, even though the participants appear extremely civilized throughout, never abandoning their decorum or mussing their formal clothes. (Yet one can fully accept the proceedings as aesthetic, ritualistic

A honeymoon journey on the Orient Express is interrupted by mysterious Dr. Werdegast—there has been a mistake in the reservations—who stares fixedly at the bride, Joan Alison (far left, below). Later, the tourist bus onto which the young couple and Werdegast have transferred overturns, and Joan is hurt (center, below). Along with Werdegast's servant, Thamal, they seek refuge in the nearby fortresslike home of Engineer Poelzig (below). Peter Alison remains concerned about his unconscious wife (left).

The secrets of Poelzig's fortress: "You are the very core and meaning of my life," he tells his wife (below). "I have cared for her tenderly and well," he says of the preserved body floating behind glass (right), and the black cat stalks menacingly through the secret passages.

Satan worship, where no clothes need be shed.) Never has Karloff had a more suavely evil role, sensuous and demonic, with his hairline pointed down the center of his forehead to make him appear like the devil himself. Rarely was Lugosi to enjoy as sympathetic a part, although by the finish he too is completely mad and caught up in the grotesque spirit of the plot.

The struggle is essentially one of good science against evil science, for

It is more than a game of chess that Poelzig plays with Werdegast. "We understand each other," he says. "We know too much of life. We shall play a little game—a game of death, if you will. . . ."

spirit of the film and culminating in actual you-are-there Satanic worship—never again so explicitly detailed in films, not even in such modern treatments of the theme as *Curse of the Demon* and *Rosemary's Baby*—makes *The Black Cat* not a Poe classic, perhaps, but a classic in the cinema of the fantastic.

Karloff, as the engineer Hjalmar Poelzig, in his strange fortress laboratory, is both scientist and modern necromancer, and indeed necrophiliac and devil worshiper as well. His struggle with Dr. Vitus Werdegast (Lugosi) takes place in an overcast middle-European mountain countryside that has a haunted and oppressive atmostphere all its own, one of brooding malevolence that creeps through every chink of our soul. This dark and spreading evil, ingrained in the

It begins on a note of happy excitement. Peter and Joan Alison are honeymooners traveling into Hungary on the Orient Express. Peter is a writer of thrillers. The compartment door opens, and Dr. Vitus Werdegast enters. There has been a mix-up over the reservations. He, like them, is going to Vizhegrad, and then on by bus. "I go to visit an old friend," he says.

Peter and Joan, their honeymoon privacy seemingly at an end, try to adjust graciously to the stranger's

81

presence. But Werdegast keeps staring at Joan. "Excuse me, but eighteen years ago I left a girl so like your lovely wife to go to war. . . . She was *my* wife. Have you ever heard of Kurgaal? It is a prison below Amsk. Many men have gone there. Few have returned. I have returned . . . after fifteen years."

Some time later the train stops, and our trio boards a tourist bus. A heavy rain is falling as they drive. The bus driver starts a friendly patter: "All this countryside was one of the greatest battlefields of the war. Tens of thousands died here. That ravine was piled twelve deep with dead and wounded men. A stream of blood ran here. And that hill yonder, where Engineer Poelzig now lives, was the site of Fort Marmaros. He built his home on its very foundations. Marmaros, the greatest graveyard in the world."

Suddenly a tree falls across their path and the bus overturns. The driver is killed, and Peter, Joan, Werdegast, and his massive servant Thamal, who had met him on the bus, must go on foot through the storm to the gates of Engineer Poelzig's fortress home.

Our first sight of the saturnine Poelzig is in his bedchamber, as he rises like a somnambulist behind a drawn curtain of veils when over an ultramodern speaker the visitors are announced. The fluted dressing gowns that appear to be his constant indoor dress fit him like dark priestly robes. He welcomes his visitors. He and Werdegast seem to be old friends—or old enemies. There is a secret they share, and when they are alone together Werdegast taunts his host. Poelzig had been the commander of Marmoros during its last terrible battle—and perhaps the man who betrayed the fort to the enemy. Why should he build his home upon its ruins? "The murderer of ten thousand men returns to the place of his crime," Werdegast cries out. "Those who died were fortunate. *I* was

Poelzig lulls the suspicions of his guests
(top left) and of the gendarmes inquiring
about the accident (center left). Thamal,
forced to obey Poelzig, attacks Peter
(bottom left) and bears him off to
imprisonment (top right). Poelzig
broodingly plays Bach on his organ.

taken prisoner. . . . Fifteen years I've
rotted. Now I've come back. Not to kill
you—but to kill your *soul*. Where are
my wife, Karen, and my daughter?"

Before Poelzig can reply, a shadow
crosses the doorway. It is of an animal,
a sleek black cat. Werdegast screams
and buries his face in his hands. Peter
and Joan hear him and enter, puzzled.
Poelzig, a sly smile on his face, offers
an explanation: "You must be
indulgent with Dr. Werdegast. He is the
victim of one of the commonest
phobias, but in an extreme form. He
has an intense and all-consuming horror
of cats."

Werdegast recovers quickly. It is late,
and all retire to their rooms. All but
Engineer Poelzig, who begins a solitary
walk through the lowest levels of his
fortress, stroking the black cat in his
arms. He moves through tunnel after
futuristic tunnel, until he comes to one
wide passageway where, within a series
of transparent displays like square
tubes, the bodies of at least half a
dozen women float either in death or
suspended animation. Poelzig pauses
before each, reflectively. Moments later,
he bursts into the darkened room where
Dr. Werdegast is sleeping. "Now, Vitus,
we have something to settle, we two!"

Unrattled, Vitus counters with,
"Where is my wife?"

Poelzig pauses a moment, then nods
his head soberly, sadly. "Very well,
Vitus." He motions the doctor to
follow him, and they begin a long
descent down massive iron stairs. "This
is still a place of death. The old
foundations are still as mined as they
ever were." They come to what was
once the chart room of the fort. In a
niche in the wall, floating behind glass,
is the preserved body of a girl. "See,
Vitus, I have cared for her tenderly and
well." It is the doctor's wife; she had
died years ago, of pneumonia.
Werdegast breaks down. "And my
child, what of her?" "Dead."

84

The massive Thamal, under
Poelzig's hypnotic control, holds
Joan Alison, shortly to be sacrificed
in an unholy mass offered to Satan
by Poelzig, high priest of a
devil-worshiping cult.

Poelzig slowly leads the broken doctor from the crypt, and as the camera follows the twisting stair upward as if from the actor's viewpoint, we hear Poelzig's voice purr seductively: "Come, Vitus, are we men or children? Are we not both as much victims of the war as those whose bodies have been torn asunder? . . . And now you come playing at being an avenging angel. We understand each other. We know too much of life. We shall play a little game—a game of death, if you will. . . ."

Poelzig retires to his veiled bedroom. A woman stirs in her sleep; he touches her briefly and lies beside her. "You are the very core and meaning of my life. No one shall take you from me. Not even Vitus, your father."

A book lies by the bed. It is *The Rites of Lucifer.*

Morning floods the futuristic fortress home with rectangles of sunshine. Joan Alison seems recovered from the unsettling effects of the previous night's bus accident, and Poelzig is once again the perfect host. But his eyes linger too long on the girl . . . and Vitus notices Poelzig's interest. Vitus pulls him over to an ornate chess table for a private chat. "You plan to keep her here!" he accuses.

Poelzig seems suavely, supremely self-confident. "Tonight is the dark of the moon. Do you dare play chess for the girl?" he asks quietly.

Vitus accepts. And loses.

At that moment Peter and Joan, baggage in hand, descend the staircase and head toward the main entrance. They thank Poelzig, but they have stayed in the house long enough; they will make for a hotel in the valley, walking if necessary. With a smile, Poelzig signals. The massive servant Thamal, now for a time obeying Poelzig, strikes Peter a savage blow on the back of his head; he falls to the ground. Joan screams and faints.

Servants carry both back upstairs. All the while, Vitus looks on helplessly, for he has lost his wager. He can only be a passive player in the dark games to come.

For hours, until darkness falls over the mountains, Poelzig plays Bach on the great organ in the main room. The fortress reverberates with the solemn music. Upstairs, however, Vitus has let himself into the room in which Joan is being held prisoner and assures her that he is on her side. Poelzig is a mad beast; they must bide their time. "Did you ever hear of Satanism, the worship of the devil, of evil? Poelzig is the great modern priest of this ancient cult, and tonight, the dark of the moon, the rites of Lucifer will be celebrated. If I am not mistaken, they intend for you to play a part in the ritual!" Joan is terrified; Vitus cautions her to be brave.

A little later Joan has another visitor, one she has never seen before. A beautiful blond girl steps into the room by accident and is surprised to see Joan there. She identifies herself as Karen Poelzig. The great engineer—in Hungary *engineer* is a title equivalent to *general* in the rest of Europe—had married her mother and, some years after her mother's death, married her. Her father, Vitus Werdegast, had perished in the destruction of Marmaros when she was still a small girl. No, Joan cries, that isn't true: her father is alive, and looking for her! At that moment Poelzig steps into the room and holds the door open for Karen to leave. She does so, quickly and wordlessly. The door closes. Later, Joan hears muffled cries.

A fierce wind hurls menacing clouds across the night sky; the mountains are overcast. Strange guests begin to arrive at Fortress Marmaros. They are in evening dress—the men in black, the women in white. They gather in the main hall, before a plain but expressionistic altar over which looms what appears to be a large double cross, overturned. Hjalmar Poelzig, dressed in a black robe with a large collar, is their priest, intoning in Latin the words of the Black Mass. Joan is carried screaming up to the high altar and, fainting upon the altar, falls between the beams of the cross. As the congregation looks on intently, Poelzig, chanting, offers her soul—and body—to Satan.

The service builds to a crescendo, and one of the women worshipers faints from excitement. Seizing the diversion, Vitus and his servant, the giant Thamal (now freed from his hypnotic alignment with Poelzig), who had both been hiding behind the altar, grab Joan from the cross and make their way down the twisting metal stairs to the subterranean tunnels. There Thamal kills one of Poelzig's servants but is himself mortally wounded. There, too, Joan manages to tell Vitus that Karen is still alive—and married to his nemesis!

The news of his daughter drives Vitus berserk. And then, with an agonizing cry, he sees, in an underground laboratory, the body of a girl. It is Karen.

Poelzig rushes down the metal stairs. Vitus hurls himself upon him, with the strength of a madman. The dying Thamal helps Vitus suspend his enemy from a rack and strip him of his robes. *Do you know what I am going to do with you now? Did you ever see an animal skinned? That's what I'm going to do—tear the skin from your body . . . slowly . . . bit by bit!"* From a surgical table in the lab Vitus snatches a scalpel and, laughing maniacally, begins his grisly revenge. Joan screams.

Peter, who has somehow escaped from the cell in which they had placed him and armed himself with a revolver, dashes through the tunnel and fires on Vitus Werdegast.

Sinking to the floor, Vitus manages to say, "You poor fool . . . I was only trying to help. Now go . . . please go. . . ." As Peter and Joan flee up the stairs, Vitus crawls to a set of massive switches set in the wall. Grabbing one, he turns to the torn body of Poelzig. "Five minutes—and this switch ignites the dynamite. Five minutes and Marmaros, you and I, this whole rotten cult will be no more. . . ."

Peter and Joan dash out of the fortress and make their way to the road below. Behind them, the sky itself seems to ignite as Marmaros erupts, a second after Vitus Werdegast's final words: "It has been a good game, Hjalmar. . . ."

The Black Cat does not make sense in a number of departments. For what bizarre reason does Engineer Poelzig have several women suspended in his subterranean display cases? Has Vitus's morbid fear of cats been introduced into the plot for any other purpose than a casual link with Poe? And we can only guess at the steps that led Poelzig from being both a leader and later a traitor on the field of battle to being high priest of a Satanist cult.

Despite these questions, *The Black Cat* was extremely popular, so much so that Universal was moved the following year to cast Bela Lugosi and Boris Karloff together again in *The Raven.* In this film Lugosi had more of a chance to be center stage, portraying a plastic surgeon so obsessed with the works of Edgar Allan Poe that he builds several of Poe's more intriguing torture devices. Karloff plays the character role of a gangster whose face Lugosi—claiming he is disguising—hideously scars. It falls far short of *The Black Cat*, possibly because Edgar G. Ulmer did not direct it. Ulmer did very little for Universal and moved in the forties to small independent studios. There for the next decades he directed such melodramas as

Bluebeard (1944) and *The Man from Planet X* (1951), and, in the early 1960s in Europe, a new and very interesting version of *Queen of Atlantis.* In the past few years a "camp" cult has risen around his work, especially the B movies he did in the forties for such small but energetic Hollywood studios as Monogram. Good as these small but pretentious dramas were—and they were all dark and brooding—the cult that embraced Ulmer's work should have placed his *Black Cat* right at the top.

For *The Black Cat,* with its weird and terrifying clashes between good and evil, is one of the most genuinely horrific films of the genre. It is a clear adaptation of the Germanic stylized horror of the previous decade, the closest the American screen was to come to it. There are no monsters in the film of the kind that Universal had previously so successfully exploited. Even the black cat of the title makes only a minimal and incidental appearance, so far removed from the core of the plot that no one even

Berserk, Werdegast begins to strip the skin from the suspended body of his enemy. . . .

bothers to give it a name. Neither Karloff nor Lugosi is in any way a supernatural creature, yet the obsessions that drive them—revenge, Satan worship—bring them into a conflict upon a landscape so evil it makes us shudder. It is not the devil worship itself that is terrifying—although this was novel ground for film-makers, the congregation is cautiously presented as impeccably mannered—it is the fear and dread that hang, as oppressive as a storm cloud, over the battlements of Marmaros, the futuristic fortress built over the massive grave site. Few films have ever managed to generate such dread, and in such a stylish and shadowy way. That *The Black Cat* succeeds so singularly well makes it a memorable addition to the cinema of fantastic horror.

THE BRIDE OF FRANKENSTEIN

The Monster	Boris Karloff
Henry Frankenstein	Colin Clive
Elizabeth	Valerie Hobson
The Mate/Mary Shelley	Elsa Lanchester
Doctor Praetorius	Ernest Thesiger
The Hermit	O. P. Heggie
Karl	Dwight Frye
Burgomaster	E. E. Clive
Minnie	Una O'Connor
Shepherdess	Ann Darling
Percy Bysshe Shelley	Douglas Walton
Lord Byron	Gavin Gordon
Rudy	Neil Fitzgerald
Hans	Reginald Barlow
Hans's wife	Mary Gordon
A Hunter	John Carradine

Directed by James Whale
Produced by Carl Laemmle, Jr.
Screenplay by William Hurlbut
Adapted by William Hurlbut and John L. Balderston from events in the
    1816 novel by Mary Wollstonecraft Shelley
Editorial supervision: Maurice Pivar
Music by Franz Waxman
Photography: John D. Mescall
Editor: Ted Kent

Released (and originally to be titled *The Return of Frankenstein)*
    by Universal May 6, 1935.

He was tall and thin, yet extremely graceful. Much of his sardonic, "black" humor was lost upon his audiences, who came to his horror films to be frightened and were not disappointed. He once directed a war story dressed throughout the shooting in the uniform of a German officer, with his camera crew sporting those of lesser ranks. His contribution to the cinema of the fantastic is enormous, for he single-handedly pulled the switch that brought the dead to life and began the horror film's foremost dynasty. He was James Whale, and not only did he father Frankenstein's monster, he mated him as well.

Whale was born of working-class parents in a small English town. A soldier in World War I, he was captured by the Germans and developed a taste for acting and directing while doing shows for diversion in a prisoner-of-war camp. When he was released, he continued acting in various repertory companies, and in 1928 he had the opportunity to direct R. C. Sherriff's startling antiwar play *Journey's End* on the London stage. (No one else wanted the job, for the pay was too small.) The play, an instant success, was brought to New York, and ultimately—in 1930—Whale directed the screen version of it in Hollywood for Tiffany Pictures. He proved very facile with his camera, and the film—especially his directorial work—won wide praise.

Impressed by the camera work of this smooth Englishman who also had, in this early sound period, a stage background in dialogue, Universal Studios hired him to direct a sentimental story about the tragic love of a London prostitute and a soldier, *Waterloo Bridge* (1931). It, too, was a success. Universal then gave him a choice of several projects. Whale selected *Frankenstein*—offered to him partially because it was felt he would be good at handling its European

atmosphere—because, of all the available properties, "it was the strongest meat and gave me a chance to dabble in the macabre. I thought it would be amusing to try. . . ."

Mary Wollstonecraft Shelley's early-nineteenth-century novel had already interested silent-film makers: in 1910 a quick version had been cranked out at the New Jersey Edison studios. After the enormous public response to Universal's 1931 screen version of the smash Broadway vampire thriller *Dracula,* for which studio head Carl Laemmle had imported Bela Lugosi, he rightly guessed that a surge in interest in horror films was on the way and could be exploited. Bela Lugosi had already made a test as the monster in *Frankenstein* under the talented and very individualistic director Robert Florey, but it had not worked out. Bela was unhappy that his face would be almost unrecognizable under heavy makeup—based in the test on the makeup used in the German film version of *The Golem,* about a giant clay figure brought to life—and that he would be mute throughout the drama.

The directorial assignment then passed to James Whale. Although Leslie Howard—who had just completed *Outward Bound* (1930), a fantasy film about passengers aboard a fog-bound ship slowly realizing they are all dead—had been considered for the title role of young Dr. Frankenstein, Whale rejected him in favor of Colin Clive. Earlier he had cast Clive (who was then in a chorus line) as the lead first in the stage version of *Journey's End* (replacing, interestingly enough, Laurence Olivier) and then in the film version.

But who was to play the monster Frankenstein had created—a role rather secondary to the scientist's part, at least as conceived by the script? Whale chose another Englishman, an angular, middle-aged actor with an interesting face whom he had seen play a snarling convict in a road-company presentation of *The Criminal Code.* Boris Karloff had been in films for more than a decade, rarely playing more than bits and walk-ons, although in 1926, in a silent film called *The Bells,* he portrayed a mesmerist with striking similarities to Caligari. Whale was fascinated by Karloff's tough, craggy face and penetrating gaze, but no one responded more to its potential than Jack Pierce, Universal's ace makeup man. Pierce made exhaustive studies—consulting surgeons and watching autopsies—of what a being created out of sewn-together corpses might actually look like. Taking his cue from Karloff's bony forehead, Pierce fashioned the top-heavy skull, then added green skin, scars, electrodes. Boots and a built-up body made the somewhat frail Karloff appear a creature of towering, crushing strength, but far more forceful than his hulking shape was what Whale called Karloff's "queer, penetrating personality." It would win over a world.

Frankenstein explored a very powerful theme, and for a time Universal executives were afraid public reaction might be unfavorable. Henry Frankenstein, a young medical student given to experimenting with electricity and with rays beyond the ultraviolet range—the very forces that may be the creators of life—works in a secret laboratory in an old watchtower. One stormy night, as he draws power from the lightning-charged heavens, he stirs into life the being he has manufactured out of many cadavers. "It's alive," he shouts in maniacal glee, "It's alive! . . . *How like a God . . .*" (This line was deleted from later reissues of the film.) Unfortunately, having given life to the creature, Henry is ill prepared for what he will do with it next; his hunchbacked servant whips it, while his astonished professor wishes to

dissect it. Both the latter provoke the creature until it kills them—more out of terror than vengeance—and escapes into the forests and villages of the mid-European locale.

Even though the monster accidentally kills a small girl by a mountain lake, at no time does our sympathy fail to go out to this bewildered, hurt creature, this newborn, suffering giant. Clearly Henry Frankenstein, through his irresponsibility, is the guilty one, and when the monster blunders into Henry's baronial home and nearly kills his bride-to-be, it is almost an act of retribution. A mob of villagers drives the creature to an old mill, however, where it finally manages to vent its fury upon its creator by hurling Henry from the top of the structure. (Henry falls on a blade of the windmill and is saved.) The villagers set fire to the mill, and the creature perishes.

One of the most successful films of the decade and even of all time (it is still earning money for its studio), *Frankenstein,* released late in 1931, no doubt reflected the uncertainties of the early Depression years by binding all the nameless fears of the period into one grotesque yet not altogether repulsive being. As in the real world, here was one more experiment gone amok. This theme of the scientist who creates forces he then cannot control was molded by *Frankenstein* and shaped the future of the horror cinema.

Undoubtedly the unsettled early thirties needed exactly this sort of shock stimulus; however, much of *Frankenstein*'s success is due to Boris Karloff's sensitive, powerful performance. In spite of this, it took some time for his contribution to be recognized by the studio. He was not important enough to be invited to the film's premiere! The public, on the other hand, took Karloff to heart at once, even linking his role with the

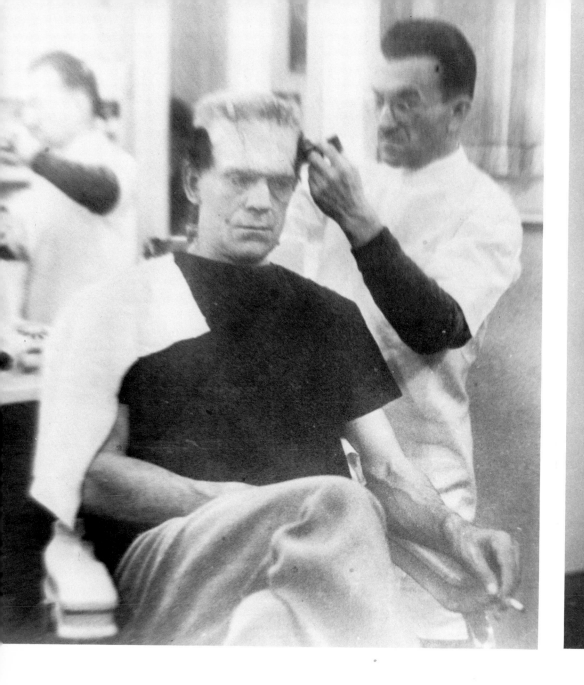

The great makeup genius Jack
Pierce puts the finishing touches to
the monster whose visage he
shaped.

film's title, although his monster was
nameless throughout and the title
referred to the part played by Colin
Clive. Suddenly, at forty-two, with
years of thankless parts behind him,
Karloff had become a star.

James Whale's stock had risen
considerably too, and he went on to do
other melodramas and fantasies for
Universal. *The Old Dark House* (1932)

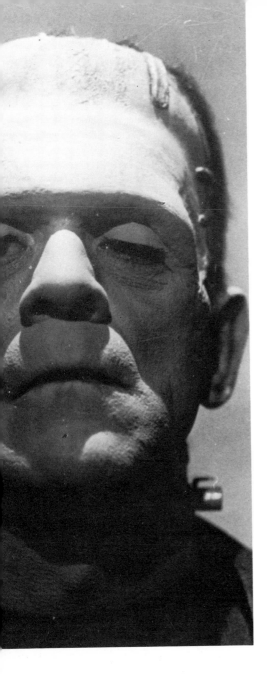

is a superior thriller about strangers obliged by a storm to take shelter in a decaying, mysterious old mansion, where Karloff is the mute, bearded butler. H. G. Wells's *The Invisible Man* (1933), which starts with an English rural community terrorized by a bodiless being (Claude Rains, not seen until the film's closing shot), is a landmark of science fiction.

By the mid-thirties, however, Universal had begun to regret that it had disposed of its premier monster—the film was still earning enormous sums of money—and so it gave James Whale the opportunity to surpass himself in a sequel, *The Bride of Frankenstein.* In this new film Karloff was again cast in the role that had brought him fame, and Elsa Lanchester, the English actress who excelled at playing eccentrics and had won world acclaim as one of the wives in *The Private Life of Henry VIII* (1933), was added to accommodate the new pivotal dilemma: creating a mate for the monster, a female for its species.

Whale's creative and artistic controls over the film are constantly in evidence, from its eerie, oppressive atmosphere to its often outrageous graveside humor. A sardonic wit intrudes on nearly every scene, even the most macabre; it is Whale winking at us. And, just as the central theme of his first film caused the more timid Universal executives to worry about offending large segments of their audiences, Whale in the sequel went even further in deliberately ruffling spiritual sensitivities: the monster overturns religious statues and appears to rail against God in heaven. But it is precisely these touches that bring *The Bride of Frankenstein* to a very high level of the cinema of the fantastic. Surpassing its predecessor, it remains the best film of the Frankenstein series. It is certainly James Whale's best film, and it stands as the best monster film of its own decade and of several others.

The Bride of Frankenstein contradicts the ending of its earlier version, which had left Henry Frankenstein quite fit after his ordeal, and ready again to exchange marriage vows. (It also changed wives on him, substituting the glamorous young

93

Valerie Hobson, then only eighteen, for Mae Clarke in the role.) The plot of the second film begins at the burning mill, with both the monster and his maker seemingly lost.

More precisely, the film begins with Mary Wollstonecraft Shelley herself, introducing this continuation of her literary creation, for, in a unique and interesting prologue, Whale brings his own author on stage, thereby providing another role and double duty for Elsa Lanchester. She is the youthful Mary Shelley, chatting cosily with the elegant Lord Byron and Percy Bysshe Shelley on a stormy night. Byron chides her for writing a tale of monsters, but Mary corrects him: "My purpose was to write a moral lesson, of the punishments that befell a mortal man who dared to emulate God." And there is more to the story. Byron and Shelley gather eagerly around her as the girl returns them to the burning mill. . . .

The monster is not dead after all; he has fallen through the flaming rafters into an underground cistern. From this watery retreat he makes a murderous escape, killing two villagers in his flight. (In a bizarre Whale touch, they are the parents of the child the creature had accidentally killed in the first film.) The unstoppable, unkillable creature moves into the forest.

Meanwhile, Henry Frankenstein's broken body—injured in his fall from the top of the mill—is carried home to his elaborate Gothic castle, somewhat expanded since the first film, as the budget for this new production was lavish enough to provide great stone battlements and vaulted ceilings. In the days that follow, Henry mends, but his spirit is uneasy. "I've been cursed for delving into the mysteries of Life. . . ." Had he gone against God by discovering the secret of which God is so jealous? Or was it part of the Divine Plan for him to breed a race of men and probe the mystery of *eternal* life? "No!"

94

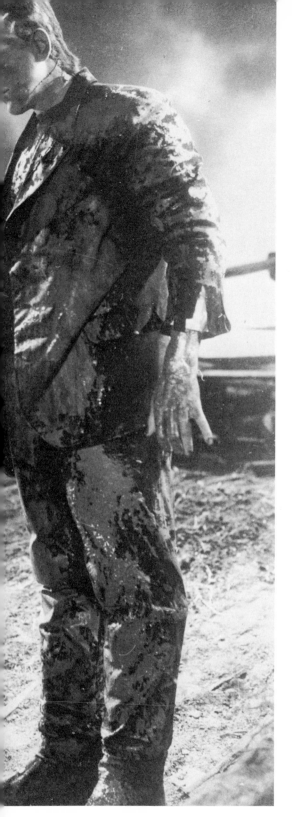

The monster rises from the ashes of
the mill, frightening a servant of
Henry Frankenstein's fiancée,
Elizabeth, (left) and killing a villager
(top), as Henry's fiancée finds a
spark of life in him.

Elizabeth, his fiancée, protests in near frenzy. There are things not meant to be known; she has dreamed of a dark shape coming to claim Henry, drawing closer and closer. . . . There is a fierce knocking at the door, announcing one of Whale's most whimsical and memorable creations, the eccentric scientist Dr. Praetorius.

The waspish, skeletal English actor Ernest Thesiger, then in his fifties, had made his film debut three years before in Whale's *The Old Dark House.* Thesiger and the director were good friends, and it was Whale's inspiration to use him to provide the Frankenstein saga with the right touch of the lightly sinister, Whale's own sense of macabre comedy. Praetorius, part genius and part charlatan, his tall, brittle body casting evil shadows, is the force to bring Henry Frankenstein back to his laboratory—back to creating monsters.

We learn Praetorius was once a doctor of philosophy at his university, but he was dismissed for knowing too much. "We must work together to reach a goal undreamed of by Science!" He has spent the last twenty years in secret experimentation and—in a somewhat different fashion—has also succeeded in creating life. Tremendously stimulated, Henry rides through the night to Praetorius's garret home. The aged scientist suggests a partnership, as he reaches for a bottle. "Do you like gin? It is my only weakness." His eyes crazed, he offers a toast. "To a new world, of gods and monsters!" Then he shows Henry his creations.

They are tiny, delicate, perfectly formed creatures: little beings in glass bottles, dressed as such Establishment figures as a king and an archbishop.

Doctor Praetorius's tiny creations: mermaid, devil, baby, ballerina, bishop, and king. (The queen is not seen in this composite still, and the baby was later left out.)

97

Mary Shelley holds Lord Byron and Percy Bysshe Shelley spellbound (top left) with her tale of the monster, who is dismayed at frightening a peasant girl in the forest—and then briefly captured.

"Do you think I'm mad?" Praetorius rasps over his living mannikins. "While you were digging in your graves, piecing together dead tissues, I went for my raw material to the source of life—I *grew* my creatures, like cultures, from seed." And Praetorius suggests they collaborate together to give Henry's monster a female mate, thus creating a man-made race upon the face of the earth!

Quite unaware of what is being planned for him, Frankenstein's creation, much of his face burnt away

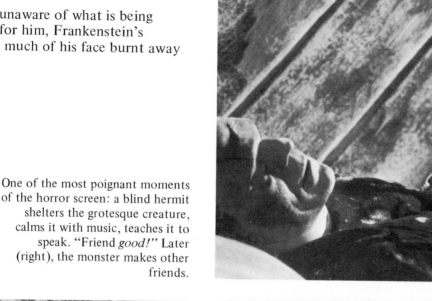

One of the most poignant moments of the horror screen: a blind hermit shelters the grotesque creature, calms it with music, teaches it to speak. "Friend *good!*" Later (right), the monster makes other friends.

to expose the steel pinnings that hold together his skull, is pushing his way through a deep forest. He is spotted, and a mob manages to pin the awkward creature to the ground and bind him as on a crucifix to two crossed poles. They carry him in triumph to the local jail, but in the next moment he has riven his chains and escaped. There are more murders: a child, a woman, a gypsy. Wounded, driven to hysteria by the villagers' wrath, the creature flees again into the deep forest. And there, coming from a hermit's shack, for the first time he hears music: the sound of a violin.

The hermit, who is blind, cannot see the monster's grotesque features: he can only sense a soul in torment. For many years he has been lonely and has prayed to God for a friend. The ensuing sequence is the most sensitive and curious in the monster cinema: the white-bearded hermit, pure of heart, wins over—to the strain of religious music—the mute creature and welcomes him to stay, blessing the heavens for ending his loneliness. Even the monster

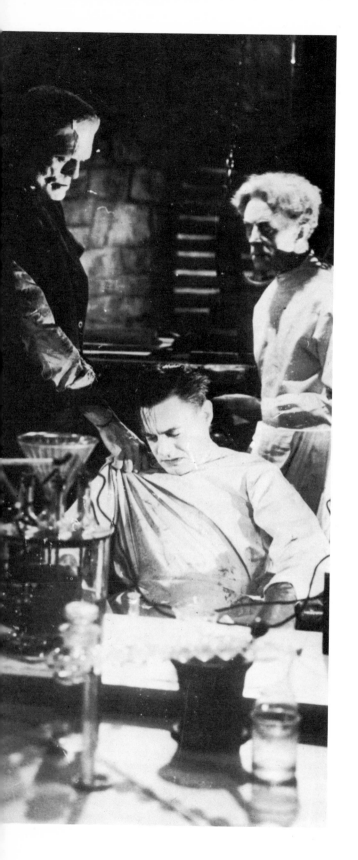

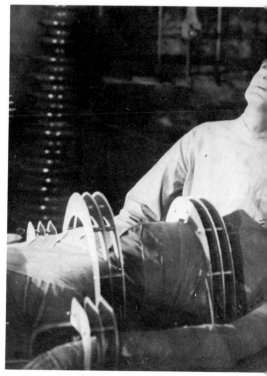

Praetorius and two gravediggers
procure the organs necessary to
create a mate for the monster (left),
while the creature makes it quite
clear to Henry Frankenstein that he
must help (far left). The laboratory
experiments begin. There is a
sputtering of electricity. Finally,
the body on the slab stirs. It is the
bride of Frankenstein. . . .

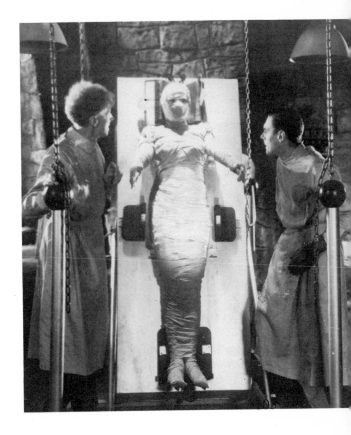

weeps. It is an incredible scene: one that only Whale could have dared.

As the weeks pass, the hermit teaches Frankenstein's creation to speak. Bread is good, wine is good; *friend* is good. But two foresters who have lost their way blunder into the hermit's hut and are aghast: "This is the fiend who has been murdering half the countryside!" They shoot at the creature, and he struggles with them; a chance spark from the fireplace sets the hut afire. The hermit's friend vanishes. It is a tragic, poignant finish to their relationship, and a supreme directorial moment for James Whale.

The monster escapes into a forest cemetery, as if to return to his origins among the dead, and there to erase himself: he topples a huge statue of a saint in mindless defiance and hides himself in an underground crypt.

But the creature is not alone. Praetorius has come to rob a grave. His two unsavory assistants have pried open the tomb of a nineteen-year-old girl and have departed, muttering that "this is no life for murderers." Praetorius, quite snug in his funereal surroundings, stays behind to enjoy a repast of cold chicken and wine. Hungry, the monster comes out of the shadows and confronts the elderly scientist, who is only momentarily startled. He begins an earnest conversation with the creature, promising he is here to make him "a woman—friend for you." The creature is pleased and moans with pleasure; a smile crosses Praetorius's face. "I think you can be very useful." His original grave-robbing chore is forgotten.

Praetorius calls on Henry Frankenstein; all is prepared for the start of their combined experiment. But Henry is now reluctant; he wants no more part in it. To Henry's horror, Praetorius opens an outer door, and in steps the monster, growling, fierce!

"Ah, yes," says the wily scientist, chuckling, "there have been improvements since he came to me." Henry crumples into a chair, still weakly refusing to continue the partnership. Praetorius signals to the monster, who lurches out. Moments later there is a scream from another part of the castle: the creature has abducted Elizabeth, Henry's bride! Now Praetorius must be obeyed.

Again we are at the old watchtower—Henry's laboratory—on a stormy night. The heart and brain from young female corpses have been assembled and put into place. Lightning draws nearer. Awaiting life, a bandaged body lies on a slab, fastened to electrodes from head to foot. Kites are released from the tower to attract electrical charges. The lab is ablaze with crackling sparks. Everywhere circuits light up in a frenzy and incandescent arcs spring from tube to tube. (It was the mad lab par excellence, the inspired creation of special-effects wizard Kenneth Strickfaden.) The slab, with the body upon it, is elevated high above the roof of the tower, where bolt after bolt of lightning strike it. Then at last it is lowered. Henry, his face tense, approaches the bandaged hand to try for its pulse. *"She's alive!"* The two scientists begin to unravel the body from its bandages.

She is a fantastic sight, a slightly grotesque approximation of the human female form. Her head is sharp-boned and angular, with few visible scars, and her cat's eyes dart about. Her hair stands straight out behind, dramatically streaked with white, both conditions no doubt the result of the lightning coursing through her body. She has been dressed in a flowing white laboratory smock, but appropriately it looks more like a bridal gown, for she is to be, as Praetorius crows in triumph, "the bride of Frankenstein!"

The creature, who has been kept in another part of the tower, enters.

In her first moment of life, the monster's mate, repelled, rejects her eager intended.

Hopefully, hesitantly, he reaches out his hand: *"Friend?"* The female screams in revulsion. There is tension in the air. He strokes her—and she springs back, screaming again. The monster's brow darkens. "She hates me. Like others." His heart broken, he begins a rampage of destruction, just as Elizabeth, who has managed to escape from her captivity, rushes into Henry's arms, pleading with him to flee. But Henry has seen the enraged monster grab for some machinery. "Don't pull that lever," he cries, "you'll blow us all to atoms!" The monster turns, and a terrible gleam of purpose fills his eyes. "You go!" he commands Henry and Elizabeth. And as they hurry from the tower, the monster turns to his mate and the cowering Praetorius. "You stay. We belong dead." He reaches for the lever, and as he pulls it, the newborn female creature directs at him one long, triumphant hiss. The watchtower is rocked by a series of tremendous explosions and topples to the ground.

The Bride of Frankenstein was the last word in monster cinema; glittering and intelligent, frightening and humorous, with the right touches of both whimsy and the Gothic macabre. But, of course, the monster, being indestructible, would not remain dead for long. In 1939 he was revived by Henry's descendant, Wolf, played by Basil Rathbone, in *The Son of Frankenstein.* It was the last time Boris Karloff was to assume the role of the creature, but the series continued beyond him, and even though the creature was portrayed by lesser hands (Lon Chaney, Jr., Bela Lugosi, and Glenn Strange) the concept rose above the players who contributed to its unending resurrections. As deathless at the box office as in the laboratory, the monster is still remembered and loved today.

Strangely, however, James Whale did not direct the third in the series, *Son of Frankenstein,* or any of the other later Frankenstein films. Shortly after his triumph with *Bride*—and after a lavish production of the Jerome Kern musical, *Show Boat* (1936), with Irene Dunne—his career took an inexplicable plunge downward. He did hardly a dozen pictures, all of them interesting, but quite secondary to his great early works, and then for years did no films whatsoever. In 1957 he was found dead in the swimming pool of his Hollywood home. He had a reserved personal life and had never married; the circumstances of his death seemed mysterious.

Boris Karloff, whom James Whale had discovered, and to whom Frankenstein's creation had brought fame, has said on more than one occasion, "My dear old monster. I owe everything to him. He's my best friend." Indeed, he's a good friend to us all.

MAD LOVE

Dr. Gogol	Peter Lorre
Yvonne Orlac	Frances Drake
Stephen Orlac	Colin Clive
Reagan	Ted Healy
Marie	Sara Haden
Rollo	Edward Brophy
Prefect Rossof	Henry Kolker
Dr. Wong	Keye Luke
Henry Orlac	Ian Wolfe
Dr. Marbeaux	Charles Trowbridge
Charles	Murray Kinnell
Françoise	May Beatty
Varsac	Rollo Lloyd

Directed by Karl Freund
Screenplay by Guy Endore
From the novel *The Hands of Orlac (Les Mains d'Orlac)* by Maurice Renard
Translated and adapted by Florence Crewe-Jones
Photography: Chester Lyons and Gregg Toland
Music: Dimitri Tiomkin
Editor: Hugh Wynn

Released by MGM July 12, 1935

The Grand Guignol was for many decades a real theater in Paris—in the rue Chaptal in Montmartre—devoted to short plays of horror and the macabre, performed in ghoulishly realistic detail. The theater gave its name to such melodrama. Bloodied love trysts, ripper murders, mob vengeance: this was the

Peter Lorre, very much at his ease in white sneakers, studies his script.

stuff of the Guignol, all elaborately, shudderingly enacted before the eyes of the audience. In 1935 Metro-Goldwyn-Mayer, still trying to ride the crest of the horror film cycle, which had largely passed that studio by, decided to use the "theater of death" as a setting in part for a fantastic tale of the medical macabre—a drama of the consequences of a hand

graft in a time when the very idea of transplants was shocking and somehow evil, a tampering with the laws of God and Nature.

The medical transplants of the cinema of the fantastic were always performed in the gleaming surgeries of mad scientists, who could be counted upon to graft souls as well as flesh. The fantasy film, with its ready stereotype of the alchemistic doctor using science as the wand to conjure his enchantments and build his power, explored futuristic themes and futuristic possibilities in ways that thrilled and frightened its audiences. Certainly hand transplants would be a medical boon of the future. Indeed, the hand graftings are performed in *Mad Love* by a surgeon who has devoted his whole life to acts of good among children, the war wounded, and the poor. And yet, what if the skilled, sensitive hands of a pianist were replaced by the hands of—a murderer? And what if a residue of soul, a trembling of the killer force, remained in those hands to influence the host body?

This was the Grand Guignol theme used by MGM in *Mad Love,* based on the classic French thriller *The Hands of Orlac,* by Maurice Renard, and previously filmed as a 1925 German silent (*Orlacs Hände)* with Conrad Veidt as Orlac and directed by

Dr. Gogol barely conceals his jealousy as a theatergoer admires the wax effigy of Yvonne Orlac.

Caligari's famed Robert Wiene. For this version MGM cast Colin Clive as the pianist Orlac. The tall, intense Clive, perhaps best known for portraying Henry Frankenstein, would this time reverse roles and be patient rather than surgeon, victim rather than experimenter. At any rate, he could portray despair and self-torture as well as anyone. For director the studio hired Karl Freund, the great German cameraman for *Metropolis* who had emigrated to this country to photograph nearly all the great horror films of Universal's golden age in the early thirties. (He had become director as well as photographer for a horror masterpiece, *The Mummy*, in 1932.)

Yvonne dresses for her final performance as an Inquisition victim (right) and receives yet one more mysterious bouquet (below). Gogol reveals himself as the sender and tries to kiss her! (below right)

With Freund they hoped to capture some of the overwhelming visual weirdness of Wiene's Germanic original; they hoped to seduce and stun the senses, as the Grand Guignol did. So they cast, in the pivotal role of Dr. Gogol, the surgeon whose "mad love" leads him to perform the transplant and orchestrate its consequences, a young Hungarian actor who had made a sensation specializing in the bizarre, an actor making his American film debut: Peter Lorre.

A short five years earlier, Lorre had been a struggling young actor at the Volksbühne (People's Theater) in Berlin, cast most often because of his short physique and round, flabby face as a troubled person or sexual deviate. Indeed, Lorre tried to exploit his physical limitations—his bulging, liquid eyes, strangely pitched voice, thickly effeminate lips, small baby face, and small round body—and best portrayed neurotics and psychopaths. At the Volksbühne one evening he was noticed

by the great German director Fritz
Lang, who at that time was toying with
the idea of filming a true Düsseldorf
police case about a child-murderer
whom the underworld aids the
authorities in catching. Lang offered
Lorre the title role of *M* (1931). ("M"
stands for the German *Mörder*,
"murderer.")

It was an incredible performance.
The actor's portrayal of the weird,
whistling child-killer, moon-faced and
harmless in appearance, pursuing his

quarry down ordinary daylight paths, tenderly hoarding a cache of children's shoes in a closet, confessing at the end before a kangaroo court of other criminals that "always someone is behind me. It is me. I want to run away. The specters are always pursuing me . . ." was the acting job of the decade, and it catapulted him to instant fame. Indeed, in an interview later, Lorre declared that once shortly after the release of *M* an angry mob stalked him down a Berlin street. He went on

Rollo, the murderer, as he is transported to the guillotine (far left), demonstrates his knife-throwing skill by hurling a pen—while handcuffed—at a train passenger. Later the inquisitive Gogol watches Rollo's execution, then relaxes at the inevitable organ (below).

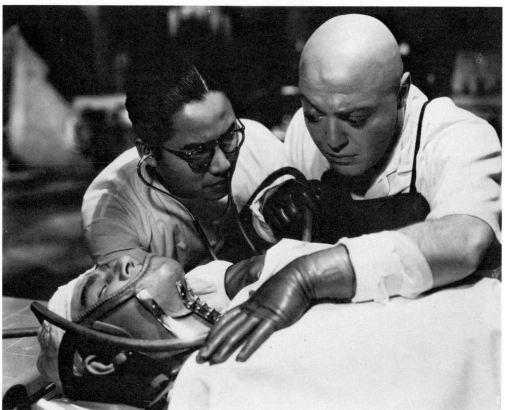

to do other roles in Germany—including the mid-Atlantic villain in the science fiction spectacle *Floating Platform One Does Not Answer (F.P.1 Antwortet Nicht,* 1933)—and did Alfred Hitchcock's *The Man Who Knew Too Much* (1934) in England. Then Columbia Pictures offered him the role of Raskolnikov, the student who senselessly kills an old woman, in Josef von Sternberg's Hollywood production of *Crime and Punishment* (1936). Lorre accepted, but before that picture began shooting he was offered the part of Dr. Gogol in *Mad Love.* It was to be his first American part. He would not get as good a role for years to come.

Mad Love tries from its first moments to be a bizarre feast for the eyes. Its credits are written on frosted glass overlooking Paris skylines; Lorre's broad shape hovers over the window, and a fist smashes the glass. Then we are inside *Le Théâtre des Horreurs,* a subterranean grotto filled with devil's heads and hanging bodies, "a place"—a girl wails—"where they make you scream and faint." Its star is the lovely, soulful-eyed Yvonne (played by Frances Drake), who has been receiving bouquets nightly from a supposedly anonymous admirer. Backstage, however, the theater is astir with the rumor that the man who sits every evening in his lonely box is the famous Dr. Gogol, who "cures deformed children and mutilated soldiers."

Yvonne learns that her husband, injured in a train wreck, may lose his hands (upper left) and begs Dr. Gogol to save them. The operation is a success (lower left), but Stephen Orlac regards his scarred, slowly healing hands with distrust.

115

Gogol, wrapped in a great fur coat—in contrast to his totally hairless head—worships Yvonne: her wax effigy at the stake in the theater lobby, her body stretched on the rack in the Inquisition scene on stage. But Yvonne loves only her husband, the famed pianist Stephen Orlac, who tonight is broadcasting his piano concerto from Fontainebleau. It is her last night at *Le Théâtre des Horreurs;* the stage is closing temporarily and she is retiring. Her husband has been on tour for a year, and this is their first real chance at a honeymoon. They have decided on a trip to England.

After the final performance, Gogol introduces himself to Yvonne. "Every night I have watched you, and tonight I felt I must come and thank you for what you have meant to me." Yvonne winces slightly when his lips touch her hand; but, in an effort at friendliness, explains she is retiring forever. Gogol is thunderstruck. "But I have come to depend upon seeing you. I *must* see you. I *must!*"

Yvonne is perplexed and somewhat frightened, but then she and Gogol are swept into a farewell party for her thrown by the cast. In the general hilarity all the actors and friends give the girl a farewell kiss. Suddenly Gogol

Orlac has a stormy scene with his father (upper left). Later the old man falls victim to a thrown knife (lower left). A reporter quizzes Gogol's housekeeper (upper right), while the doctor reassures Orlac his hands are really his.

Yvonne is repulsed by the strange doctor (above). Gogol stumbles into his surgery, haunted by phantoms of himself in the mirror that goad him to destroy Orlac and possess Yvonne. With only his eyes showing above the surgical mask, Lorre mimes distrust, horror, madness, exhaustion.

seizes Yvonne in a great bear's grasp, forcing her lips to his massive bald head. Yvonne turns away, nauseated, almost faint.

In the now dismantled lobby, Gogol buys the wax status of Yvonne for a hundred francs. He tells the foreman about the likeness of Galatea, whom Pygmalion formed out of marble. "She came to life, in his arms. . . ."

His concert finished, Stephen Orlac is on the Fontainebleau Express heading for Paris. The train is stopped at a junction, and a man in handcuffs is forced aboard. "That's Rollo—the

murderer," explains a passenger. "The American—threw knives in a circus—stopped one in his father's back because of a woman." Convicted, he is being transported to the guillotine. But fate intervenes strangely. Twenty miles outside Paris, the speeding express is derailed and goes down an embankment.

Yvonne Orlac, who had been waiting at the Paris station, rushes to the scene of the accident and rides with Stephen in the ambulance to the hospital. Now, her hysteria barely under control, she faces the doctor. "Your husband will live, madame. The head injury is not

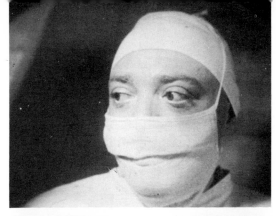
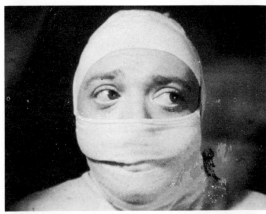
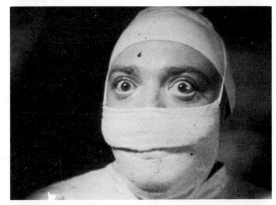

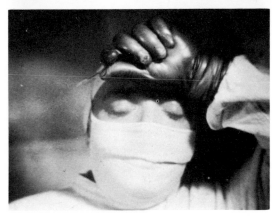

serious. It is only his hands. I'm afraid we shall have to amputate."

"Amputate?" Yvonne shrieks with despair. And then she remembers Dr. Gogol. She has heard he performs miracles on mutilated soldiers. She begs for Stephen to be taken by ambulance to Gogol's clinic.

At the clinic Gogol's round, bland

Gogol, in gruesome disguise, taunts Orlac: "They cut off my head. But Dr. Gogol put it back" (left) and urges him to arm himself (center). Later, he begins to strangle what he thinks is the wax figure of Yvonne (right).

120

face, like that of a Gargantuan baby, twitches with secret happiness when he learns that the woman he worships has asked for his aid. But Stephen's hands are doomed. "Calm yourself, madame. He is in no danger. There are other outlets for musical talent besides playing. He is also a composer. . . ." He must amputate. But Yvonne's great distress moves him. If there were only some way to help . . . Impossible, advises Dr. Wong, his associate (Keye Luke).

A sudden inspiration, however, electrifies the surgeon. He remembers Rollo, the knife-throwing murderer, whose execution he has witnessed—he watches all guillotinings—that morning. *"Impossible? Napoleon said that word was not French!"* Gogol telephones the perfect of police, and within minutes Rollo's body is rushed to the clinic.

In the next hours Gogol works feverishly in the operating room over Stephen Orlac's limbs. Then he steps back, to be congratulated by his staff. "Once I felt the blood pulsing through the hands, I knew the operation was a success." He leaves the hospital abruptly for his narrow house in a dark back street of Paris. On the uppermost floor, he plays a moody tune on a giant organ, while a mirror set in the instrument allows him to look behind him—at the wax figure of Yvonne from the Theater of Horrors.

Months pass. Stephen is recovering, but his hands are still in casts. Finally, these too are cut away. "They—they feel dead. . . ." Gogol assures Stephen this is because they have been atrophied from lack of use. "But they don't look like my hands," Stephen complains. "You forget they were badly crushed," Gogol responds. Yvonne says to the doctor, gratefully, "No one but you could have performed this miracle."

It is, however, a slow miracle, and a very expensive one—endless ultraviolet treatments and massages—and Stephen can no longer really play the piano. He

must learn all over again, like a child. Bills are pilling up; Yvonne has sold all her jewelry and they have reached the limit of their credit. They would go for aid to Stephen's father, a well-to-do jeweler, but long ago father and son were estranged when Stephen deserted the family trade for a career in music. Orlac is at his wits' end. He no longer practices the piano but listens moodily to his old records. Slowly his numb hands begin to tingle with feelings of their own. . . .

An agent comes to repossess the piano, and Stephen hurls a sharp-pointed pen into the woodwork behind his head. He visits his father in his shop, and they quarrel. He seizes a display knife and throws it into the wall.

Yvonne notes the changes in Stephen and begs Gogol to tell her the truth: will he ever play again? Instead of answering her, the surgeon says mournfully, "Your thoughts are only for him. Is there no room in your heart—even pity—for a man who has never known the love of a woman, but who has worshiped you ever since the day he walked past that absurd little theater?" Yvonne, sobbing, pleads with him to stop: "Even if I didn't love Stephen, there is something about you that—frightens me. . . ." Gogol, his eyes swelling with tears and hurt, withdraws.

Days later, Orlac bursts into Gogol's surgery. He has seen the doctor who first attended him after the train accident and has learned that his hands had been past saving. *Whose hands are these?* he demands. "They seem to have a life of their own. *They feel for knives* . . . and know how to throw them! They want to *kill!*" Gogol assures Stephen that his hands are his own, that the shock of the wreck and his injuries have left him in a shaken mental state. But privately Gogol thinks: What if Orlac *should* go mad?

From this point, the film itself seems to lose a measure of sanity. It accelerates at an unsteady pace into a mad twilight. In a fantastic German Gothic sequence, Gogol stumbles from an unfinished operation into his surgery, unable to continue, while haunting images of himself rush up at him from his own mirror, surround him, goad him: *"Nothing matters but Yvonne!"* A suave, dapper doppelgänger moves up to advise him. "The power of suggestion . . . Use it! Orlac is a weakling anyway!"

The next day Stephen's father is found in his shop, murdered. Stephen's recent quarrel with the old man—and his hurling of the knife—is remembered.

In the meanwhile, Stephen receives a telephone call. He will learn the truth about his hands if he will come to a certain address. There, in a dark room in a crumbling back street, a shadowy, cloaked figure waits for him, as motionless as a monstrous puppet wrapped in cloth. The figure speaks. "Your hands . . . they throw knives. Your hands were once mine. *I have no hands."* Stephen moans, for attached to the stranger's wrists are sets of incredible artificial fingers made of gleaming tubular steel.

It is too much for Stephen's mind to grasp. He has been in a daze and he cannot remember anything. The figure tells Stephen he has killed his own father and then drives a thick-bladed knife into the table before him. "Use this when they try to arrest you." Stephen recoils, horrified. "Who are you?" he pleads.

"I am Rollo."

"But Rollo died on the guillotine!"

The figure moves to stand, jerkily. "Yes, they cut off my head. *But Dr. Gogol put it back."* The steel fingers reach up and pull away the cloak. A thick, leather-belted steel harness fastens the head to the neck! A face we can barely see—concealed by chin-harness, dark glasses, and a hat pulled low—bursts into insane laughter as Stephen rushes from the room.

Stephen Orlac has hurled the knife that has saved his wife, and Dr. Gogol lies dying. . . .

It is one of the most frightening moments in the cinema of the fantastic.

And yet it is completely based on sham. We recognize at once that it is Gogol under the elaborate disguise, that it is a "dressing-up," a pretense in much the same league as the false blood and gore of the Grand Guignol. But, once we are over the momentary speculation that this might indeed be a resuscitated Rollo, we are hit with a second and greater shock: the bizarre extreme to which Gogol has gone to drive his quarry mad.

Stephen Orlac is arrested for his father's murder. Distraught, and sensing something of the truth, Yvonne makes her way into Gogol's home, thinking him at the clinic, and is trapped when he returns unexpectedly, still in his fantastic steel gloves and neck, crowing with triumph. "The power of suggestion—it worked! They will put him away . . . while it is *I* who am mad!" For a moment Yvonne avoids discovery by taking the place of her own wax statue, but she trembles as Gogol comes close to her. "Galatea!

123

You came to life in my arms! Give me your lips. . . ." He tries to make love to her, but driven by the voices and dark shapes of his nightmare, he is strangling her.

Happily, however, Stephen has managed to convince the police that Dr. Gogol is somehow involved in the murder. They arrive at the doctor's house just in time to rescue Yvonne—as Stephen with his scarred right hand tosses a knife square into Gogol's back. The film's final shot is of Gogol sinking to the floor, a victim of the deadly aim he had himself grafted upon the pianist Orlac.

The director of *Mad Love,* Karl Freund, was never to direct another film, but as one of the world's great cinematographers he remained very active, especially in television, until his recent death. For Peter Lorre, very few roles thereafter were to bring him so close to center stage. His specially shaven head accentuating his bulging eyes, his soul-piercing anguish throbbing through such lines as "I—a poor peasant—have conquered science; why cannot I conquer love?" made his portrayal of the iconoclastic scientist suddenly exposed to and destroyed by

human emotion a classic of its kind. Most of his parts in the years immediately following were confined to B quickies, although, as in the Mr. Moto series, he tried to make the most of them. Then, in 1941, he was paired with Sydney Greenstreet in *The Maltese Falcon,* and the success of the combination led, for Lorre, to a Warner Brothers contract and roles of stature once more. Oddly enough, he was rarely to play a scientist again.

Mad Love has been filmed at least twice since. In the 1964 Mel Ferrer version Gogol is done away with entirely and Christopher Lee, as a sort of paranoid stage magician, takes on the villain's part. The cinematic image of the surgeon daring and sinister enough to experiment with transplants is fading; today severed hands are sewn back on without a second's thought. Of course, *Mad Love* is concerned not with hands but with souls, and whether some of a murderer's strength and character and evil can be grafted onto another. And it explores an even more traditional theme, one that is curiously satisfying: that even wise men can be driven mad by love.

FLASH GORDON

Flash Gordon	Larry "Buster" Crabbe
Dale Arden	Jean Rogers
Emperor Ming	Charles Middleton
Princess Aura	Priscilla Lawson
Dr. Zarkov	Frank Shannon
Prince Barin	Richard Alexander
King Vultan	John Lipson
High Priest	Theodore Lorch
Professor Gordon	Richard Tucker
King Thun	James Pierce
King Kala	Duke York, Jr.
Zona	Muriel Goodspeed
Shark Man	House Peters, Jr.
Tigron's Mistress	Sana Rayya
Monkey Men	Constantine Romanoff
	Bull Montana

Episodes
1. The Planet of Peril
2. The Tunnel of Terror
3. Captured by Shark Men
4. Battling the Sea Beast
5. The Destroying Ray
6. Flaming Torture
7. Shattering Doom
8. Tournament of Death
9. Fighting the Fire Dragon
10. The Unseen Peril
11. In the Claws of the Tigron
12. Trapped in the Turret
13. Rocketing to Earth

Directed by Frederick Stephani
Produced by Henry MacRae
Screenplay by Frederick Stephani, George Plympton, Basil Dickey, Ella O'Neill

Based on Alex Raymond's comic strip
Photography: Jerry Ash and Richard Fryer
Music from classical themes and from Franz Waxman's score for
  The Bride of Frankenstein
Art Director: Ralph Berger
Electrical effects: Norman Drewes
Editors: Saul Goodkind, Edward Todd, Alvin Todd, Louis Sackin

Released by Universal April 6, 1936

He was called the American Siegfried, and with cause. He fought sorcerers and dragons in kingdoms as spired as those on a tapestry, in tales of interplanetary voyages that have all the ring of medieval epics. Flash (he has no other first name) is the noblest of all film heroes. Full of manly grace and pure of heart, he flings himself against a menace suspiciously oriental. A laughing Nordic superman, he protects humanity from the slant-eyed, yellow-skinned Emperor Ming, who guides an aggressor planet hurtling into our orbit to destroy our lives and ways and who is a villain worthy of the Hearst chain of newspapers in which the great serial *Flash Gordon* appeared. An authentic folk hero of the twentieth century, Flash is a blond astronaut in an innocent vision of our interplanetary future; completely unfettered by impersonal technology, he substitutes instead a muscular mingling of swordplay and death ray. Futuristic, romantic, simple and direct, yet filled with strong undercurrents of sex and racial surrender, *Flash Gordon*—like its sputtering rockets—makes for the very heights of the fantastic cinema. And succeeds.

"Flash Gordon thunders into life on the screen," the Universal Studio ads blared. "With all his dragon battles, with all his sensational rocket crashes, with all his world-conquering marvels, his scientific and mechanical wonders! Leap centuries ahead of time into fantastic planetary worlds!" Flash conquered worlds and conquered the box office. Surprisingly for a low-budget venture, it was the second most profitable Universal production for 1936, outdistanced only by a much more costly Deanna Durbin A feature. It was the only serial series to be billed ahead of the features it accompanied and to be reviewed with raves by *Time*. The most glorious, exultant chapterplay ever made, it is still in demand although the serial form itself is now a dead art.

Universal Studio had always been a serial pacesetter, even in the silent days; it produced the first chapterplay with sound, *The Indians Are Coming* (1930). Its energetic production chief, a Canadian named Henry MacRae who had long been associated with serials, convinced Universal's head, Carl Laemmle, to continue chapterplays into the 1930s. Fast and inventive, the Universal serials of the early thirties might best be represented by the 1933 *Perils of Pauline,* whose round-the-world adventures were mainly drawn from newsreel footage—Shanghai street riots, Malay jungle expeditions—carefully matched with studio backlot closeups. (The Object of this globe-girdling serial? A poison gas—one that had destroyed ancient civilizations—which Pauline's scientist father is seeking "for

126

humanitarian use"!) MacRae was a master at this sort of borrowing; in every chapter of the 1935 Tarzan-style jungle serial *Call of the Savage* (for which MacRae was associate producer) there is at least one long animal fight sequence lifted from forgotten African travelogues. Rather than cheapening the Universal product, however, this grafted footage often lifted settings and story lines out of the routine, making the serials more colorful.

MacRae had long before decided that borrowing good solid stories from other media would be to the serials' advantage. Whenever possible, Universal serials were taken from established literary properties; *The Lost Special* of 1933, for instance, was based on a railroad mystery by the creator of Sherlock Holmes, Sir Arthur Conan Doyle. Then, in 1934, Universal decided to utilize as well the plots and heroes of the new art form—the newspaper adventure comic strip, fast growing in popularity. The first strip chosen for film adaptation was Hal Forrest's pioneer aviation saga, *Tailspin Tommy,* which chronicled the transformation of a small-town boy into an ace flier very much in the Lindbergh mold. It was a profitable serial for the studio and was followed the next year by a sequel, *Tailspin Tommy and the Great Air Mystery,* in which Tom fights air battles with a masked pilot in South American skies. This chapterplay also did well financially.

Universal was beginning to enjoy raiding the comics for serial heroes, for not only did the newspaper strips provide ready-made, highly visual melodrama in cliff-hanger format, they provided a ready-made audience as well. Universal decided its third adaptation would be the new and extremely well drawn adventure strip set on other planets that in two short years had caused a sensation. Its name

was *Flash Gordon,* and its creator was Alex Raymond.

Raymond had started his career as a Wall Street brokerage clerk, with no idea of ever becoming an artist. But when the 1929 crash wiped out his job, a New Rochelle neighbor—Russ Westover, creator of the *Tillie the Toiler* strip—who knew of his drawing skill encouraged him to enter cartooning professionally. Westover ultimately helped him get a position: as a $15-a-week art department assistant at King Features, the powerful syndicate that provided most of the comics for the Hearst papers. A short time later, King Features held a contest to discover an artist capable of drawing a new daily strip, *Secret Agent X-9,* a hard-hitting crime-and-spy drama created and actually written for a brief time by Dashiell Hammett. Raymond submitted some of his realistic, painstaking drawings and, surprisingly, got the job. His career as top cartoonist had begun.

Almost as soon as he had started work on *Secret Agent X-9,* Raymond submitted a sample page of a science fiction adventure comic he had been developing casually. (King Features had been looking for a futuristic strip with which to battle the fantastically popular *Buck Rogers,* started in 1929 by a rival syndicate.) It was turned down. So Raymond tried again. His hero, Yale polo champion "Flash" Gordon, was to be grounded firmly in contemporary times, unlike Buck Rogers, whose adventures were set in the twenty-fifth century, a future time to which he awoke after succumbing to a strange seeping gas in a Pittsburgh mine shaft sometime after World War I. Flash was to stay in the present, finding his excitement on other planets with futuristic cultures.

The very first panel of his new sample was a grabber: newspaper headlines scream: "WORLD COMING

TO END—STRANGE NEW PLANET RUSHING TOWARD EARTH—ONLY MIRACLE CAN SAVE US, SAYS SCIENCE!" A desperate scientist, the bearded Hans Zarkov, works day and night to avert the end of the world, but his great brain is weakening. In the next panels Flash Gordon and pretty Dale Arden, two passengers on a transcontinental plane, find their destinies joined as atmospheric disturbances caused by the onrushing comet force them to bail out of the aircraft in a shared parachute. They land near Zarkov's observatory, and he in turn, somewhat deranged, forces the couple to enter the spacecraft he has constructed nearby. "I intend to shoot this ship at the comet which threatens the Earth! My ship will deflect the comet from its course. . . . We three shall die, martyrs to science!" Surprisingly enough, the rocket, unlike the one in the later serial version, is launched vertically, much like an Apollo missile of today. "With a deafening roar, Dr. Zarkov's rocket ship, with Flash and Dale aboard, shrieks into the heavens. . . ."

In later pages the missile manages to land on the planet, whose erratic orbit takes it past Earth. The adventurers learn that the world is called Mongo and is inhabited by humanoids ruled by a despicable tyrant of yellowish cast, who looks oddly like a combination of an operatic Mephistopheles and Dr. Fu Manchu and is named Emperor Ming the Merciless. Almost immediately sides are joined and a titanic struggle is begun.

King Features liked the new format, and *Flash Gordon* debuted as a Sunday strip on January 7, 1934. Along with it, to serve as a "top piece," Raymond created *Jungle Jim* as a rival to the successful *Tarzan* strip, which also belonged to a rival distributor. (In those days the Sunday comics section had both more paper and more attention; artists of popular strips got a whole page on which to work and often invented curtain-raising companion strips, which ran as "top pieces" above their major work. Such was *Jungle Jim.*)

Both creations were immediate successes. Not only were Raymond's wild, imaginative narratives talked about, his precise and graceful drawings were the wonder of the industry. Raymond often spent as many as four days on a single Sunday page—when other artists were notoriously more slapdash. So draining were his efforts in regard to *Flash* that he was soon forced to abandon drawing *Secret Agent X-9.)* Raymond's beautiful people—both Flash and Dale were strikingly handsome—conquering fantastic worlds had an instant impact and did much to win new audiences for the adventure strip concept. Among his readers were the Universal management and Henry MacRae, hungry for new, different, ready-made heroes.

The idea of an interplanetary odyssey, of incredible cities and people, and of a popular property with a presold audience to boot, appealed to Universal, and the studio made a deal for *Flash* with King Features. (They picked up at the same time several of the syndicate's other heroes, including *Jungle Jim* and *X-9.)* With deliberate care, they scripted a faithful translation of the first year of the strip's continuity. Because such fanciful alien people as lion men and shark men had to be brought to the screen, as well as floating cities, underwater cities, and monsters of all sizes, the serial was given a total budget that ultimately reached $350,000—making it the most expensive chapterplay to date and, indeed, in the history of the form. (Some claim this figure a publicity exaggeration, but it must have been close to the true cost.) Despite this largesse, Universal indulged in some sharp economies, using bits and corners from whatever sets they felt might do, including massive Egyptian props from *The Mummy* and the laboratory and the twisting stone tower steps from *The Bride of Frankenstein*. Several of the serial's scenes, when examined closely, appear to be played quite simply against draperies and props; Vultan's throne room is a very model of starkness, for example. By spreading its money frugally yet wisely among a large number of settings and miniatures—including fleets of rocket ships, barren wastelands, cities in the sky supported by vast antigravity beams—Universal was able to produce from what was actually a fairly modest budget (for anything but a serial) a creditable epic.

The studio took as much care in choosing its stars. Raymond's characters were not only handsome and well drawn, they also had sexual problems novel and daring to the comic strip. While Flash's affection for Dale Arden was always subdued and nonphysical, there were ceaseless attempts by Other Women in the strip (generally queens, or rulers of Mongo's matriarchal kingdoms, or even Ming's daughter) to separate the lovers and claim Flash for their own. Ming expends considerable energy in the first serial trying mainly to bed but even to wed Dale Arden; he is completely taken with the earth girl, who, in a departure from the strip, is made blond as a contrast to Ming's oriental look and in order that his lust appear more alien.

As Dale the studio cast contract player Jean Rogers, who had previously been in their *Tailspin Tommy* serial and had been a New England beauty-contest winner while still in her teens. She was full of a wholesome, youthful sexiness capable of stirring any insane dictator. They gave the role of Emperor Ming to character actor Charles Middleton, who before this had often been typed as a tight-lipped rural farmer. And yet his performance as the leering, bravura, arm-waving demagogue was unforgettable enough to earn Ming a place in the gallery of great villains.

For blond, athletic Flash the studio heads chose especially carefully, since the public already had a detailed image against which to match their selection. (Among those tested for the part was Jon Hall, later to star in Universal's countless Arabian Nights spectacles and, still later, as television's Ramar of the Jungle.) They finally decided upon a young Paramount contract player (whom they arranged to borrow) named Larry "Buster" Crabbe. Not only was Crabbe good-looking and cut to Flash's heroic mold (a brunet, his hair would by dyed for the film), he had impeccable physical credentials: he had been a member of the U.S. Olympic swimming team in 1928 and 1932, setting many records and winning, in 1932, the Gold Medal for freestyle swimming. His first film role was as "Kaspa, the Lion Man" in *King of the Jungle* (1933), and he had also—for a 1933 Principal serial and feature—portrayed Tarzan in *Tarzan the Fearless*. Most of his film career until then, however, had consisted of roles in nondescript Westerns and such B college comedies as *Hold 'Em, Yale* (1935). For Buster Crabbe and *Flash Gordon* it was clearly a case of an actor and a once-in-a-lifetime part waiting to be brought together.

Today Crabbe looks back wryly at *Flash Gordon;* one feels he has never quite come out from under its shadow. "Unfortunately," he told Don Shay in an interview for the book *Conversations,* "I was a hired hand. I didn't own a piece of the serials, and that's the way the ball bounces." After more than thirty years he is still identified with the role, even though he has portrayed other comic strip heroes (Buck Rogers, Red Barry, Thunda),

The planet Mongo (above), and an
example of its larger animal life
(upper right). Its emperor, Ming,
takes an immediate shine to Dale
Arden (lower right). Flash subdues
his Mongo welcoming committee
(following pages).

appeared in dozens of Westerns (as a
running heroic character called Billy
the Kid), and even tried to sully his
good-guy image by relishing a number
of villainous roles, notably in *Swamp
Fire* (1946) and *Caged Fury* (1948). He
also did a TV series as a foreign
legionnaire. But the constant,
undiminishing popularity of the space
serials he made at the very beginning of
his career dogs him to this day,
overwhelming his identity as a person
and as an actor. Being Hero of the
Universe is a hard role to live up to, and
one has the impression—perhaps
wrongly—that he is getting tired of it.

And yet, he shouldn't be. The
ennobling process of our modern media

130

perhaps bears some resemblance in its end results to the medieval canonization of legendary crusader-saints. Somehow Alex Raymond with his pen and Buster Crabbe with his very flesh, his flaring nostrils, and his determined eyes combined to create a secular saint for their own day, Saint Flash, pure of heart and noble of spirit, battling almost impossible odds for our species and threatened way of life in the very troubled thirties. It was the sort of epic for which we hungered, and what a feast it turned out to be.

The serial *Flash Gordon* opens exactly as did the first Sunday page of the strip: the whole world is in a state of frenzy because of the oncoming planet that will soon smash it to atoms. "It is only a question of time," mutters astronomer Gordon, after peering through the great eye of his observatory. He receives a telegram from his son, Flash. "Why, he gave up his polo game just in time to board the transcontinental liner, hoping to be here with us before the end!"
Patterning its economy of scene and dialogue firmly on its comic strip origin, the serial moves right to the plane, which is being battered by atmospheric disturbance. Young Flash is aboard, and so is a very nervous Dale Arden. The aircraft is clearly in trouble: the pilot comes out of the cockpit to announce that they will attempt a landing, but anyone wishing to bail out will find a parachute under his seat. "Scared, huh?" Flash asks the pretty girl, and on impulse he grabs her in his arms so that together, sharing his chute, they leap into the turbulence. They land safely, but in strange terrain: before them, gleaming in the lightning flashes, is what appears to be a rocket ship! Out of the darkness steps a bearded, middle-aged man with a gun, who warns them, "Stop where you are!"

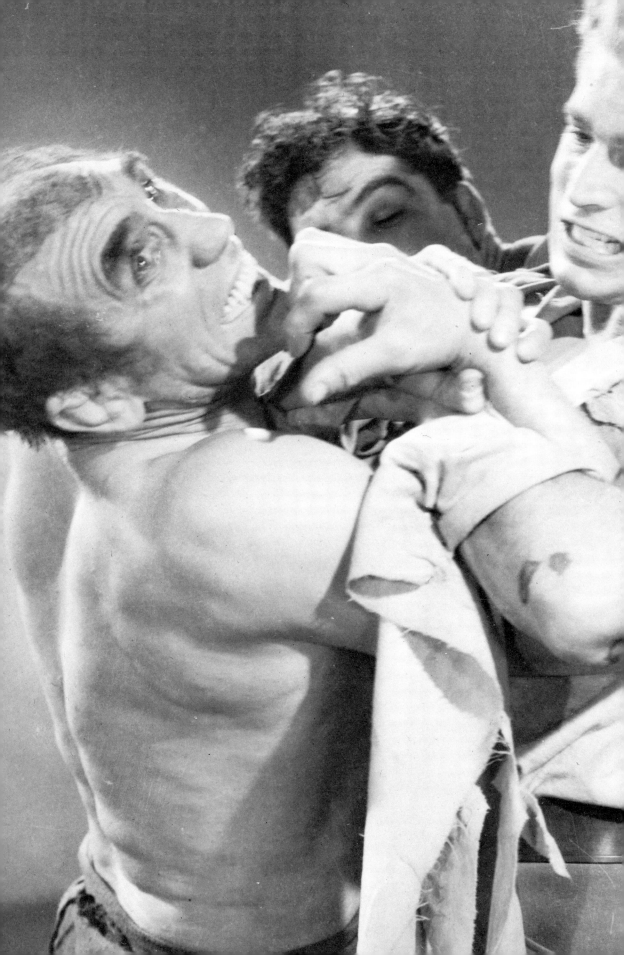

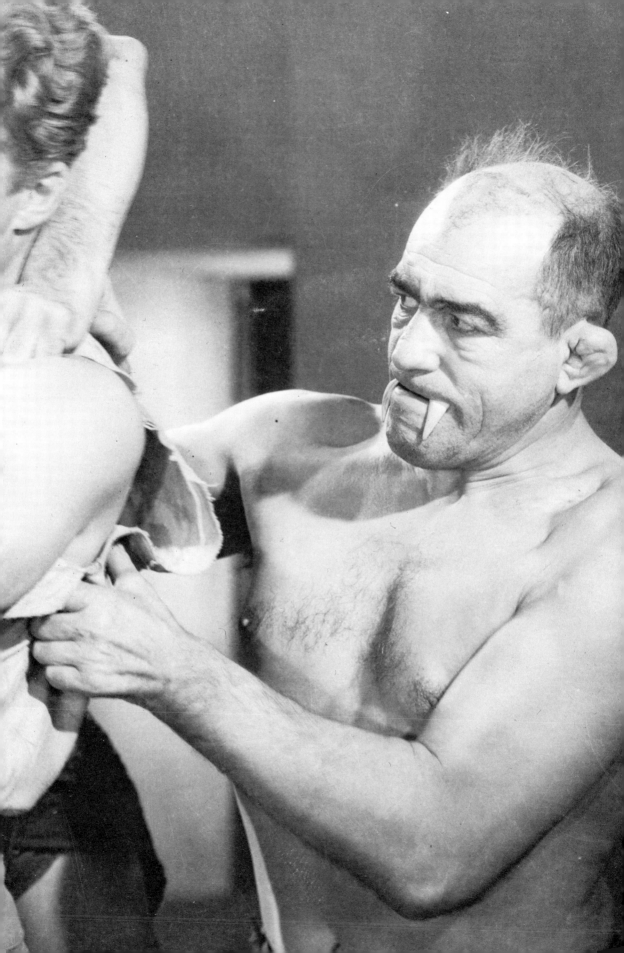

Flash immediately recognizes his father's old friend the scientist Dr. Zarkov, an eccentric with his own theories about saving Earth from the maurauding planet. The planet is inhabited, Zarkov explains hurriedly, and also "intensely radioactive"; if he can reach it with his just-completed rocket, he might perhaps be able to avert its course. "I need a man to help me—it's the only chance to save the Earth!" To strains of the Wagnerian-type music that enriches the entire serial, Flash accepts, and Dale is taken along as well on the theory there is no safe place in which to leave her

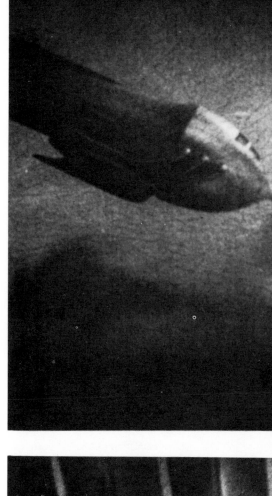

The emperor's daughter comes to Flash's rescue (below); Ming himself supervises a battle in space and admires Zarkov's scientific acumen.

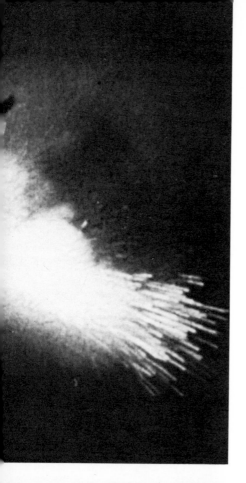

153-186-EP4

behind. With no more than a sputter of smoke, completely without runway or ramp, the tiny pear-shaped rocket belches up *horizontally*—as if from a ramp—into the violent heavens.

The trip is surprisingly brief and uneventful. In almost no time at all Zarkov announces, "We're nearly there"—and they hurtle through a Van Allen Belt-like "Death Zone." When the rocket circles to a landing on the alien planet, it is in a desolate wasteland, and the adventurers step out just in time to see a fierce battle between two giant creatures, like Earth's prehistoric reptiles, or like Gila monsters with flapping fins. Suddenly another spaceship hovers over the rocks and shoots down a ray that finishes both combatants. The ship lands, and three soldiers encased in what looks like ultramodern armor plating step out, weapons ready. "You're under arrest," they say to our friends in perfect (but unexplained) English. "You are to be taken to Ming, emperor of the Universe!" Flash attempts to resist, but Zarkov restrains him: the whole of Earth is, after all, at stake.

A throne room of fantastic opulence comes into view, and seated in its center, leaning back against an enormous gilded chair, peering from under half-closed oriental eyelids at the space visitors, is the Satanic Ming—bald, bearded, dressed in what could be a

Dale is summoned before the high priest to prepare for her marriage to Ming . . . while Flash faces a Mongo fire monster.

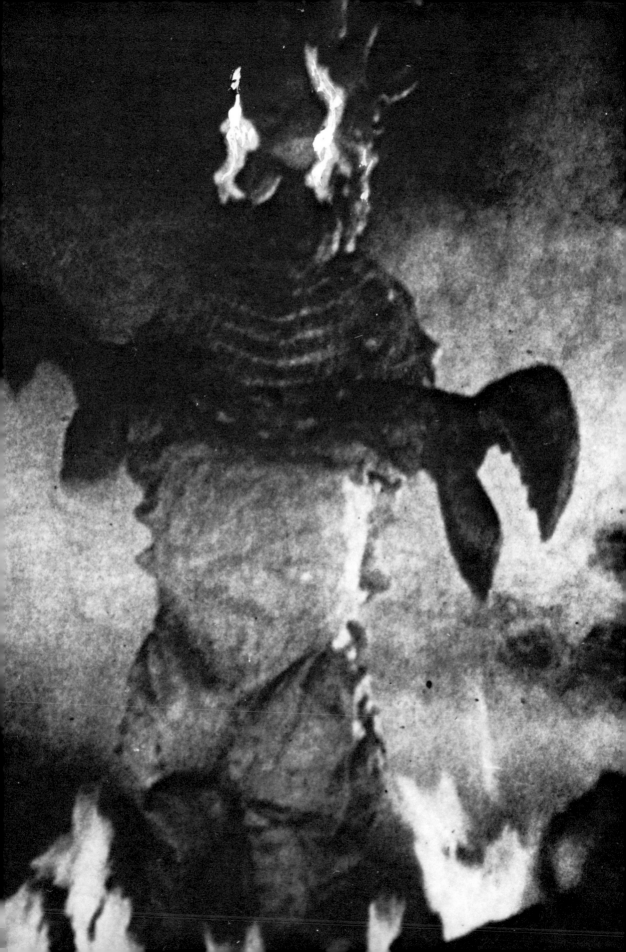

cardinal's red vestments, his face and ever-clenching tapered fingers a study in controlled fury. Zarkov explains his mission, but Ming assures him there will be no collision with Earth. "I control absolutely the movements of my planet. I will destroy your Earth in my own way." Ming immediately has Zarkov taken, a prisoner, to his laboratory. For Dale he has other plans. "Your eyes, your lips, your skin," he murmers in husky ardor; "I've never seen one like you before!" Naturally Flash jumps to Dale's defense, and it takes nearly all of Ming's palace guard to subdue him. Throw him into the arena, the emperor commands—there is a handy, caged gladiatorial area below the throne level. "He is to provide us with rare sport!"

Suddenly a dark-haired, sultry girl, regally gowned, comes up to Ming. "A bargain, Father: if he survives, *he's mine!*" She is Ming's daughter, Princess Aura, and she has been eyeing Flash with growing interest. Ming smiles, and a gong sounds. Three doors in the arena open, and from each emerges a hulking, subhuman savage, naked, fanged, and eager to fight. With only a moment's hesitation, Flash takes them all on. "He fights well, the Earthman," the emperor mutters, "but he shall not escape the pit." Horrified, Aura enters the caged arena and runs to Flash's side. "He's earned the right to live!" she cries. Ming is enraged at this sudden turn to his sport, and one of his lieutenants makes for a lever behind the

Wedding bells ring on Mongo; the Earth girl Dale is about to be plighted to the Emperor Ming.

139

throne. Pointing a ray gun, Aura downs
the soldier, who unfortunately falls
across the lever. A great black well
suddenly opens up beneath Aura and
Flash, and down its yawning mouth
they both fall. End of chapter one!

Happily, a net breaks their descent,
as we find out at the start of the second
chapter. Far below the safety of the
net, we dimly perceive a circle of
hideous reptiles. Aura has luckily found
a door in the sheer side of the pit, and
she and Flash scramble through one of
the many tunnels that riddle the planet
Mongo. From then on Flash catapults
pell-mell into one adventure after
another. He first battles and then
befriends King Thun, leader of the
Lion Men, whose great fleet of gyro
ships unsuccessfully attack Ming's
palace. Through the Lion Man's
"spaceograph"—something like an
instant TV newsreel—he sees Ming
about to marry Dale, whose mind the
fiend has clouded. Flash springs back
into the tunnels under the palace, only
to encounter an incredible monster
with great lobster claws and a
fire-spitting dragon's head. It is called a
Gocko, and Flash fights it; fortunately
Thun kills it with a ray gun.
Fortunately, too, they manage to stop
Ming's wedding just at the twelfth
sounding of a giant gong—he and Dale
would have been united at the
thirteenth stroke—and Flash escapes
with his girl to Mongo's underwater
kingdom of the Shark Men.

The geopolitical structure of Mongo
is fascinating. There are a number of
warring small kingdoms and races—the
races all seem anthropomorphic.
There are also a few very uneasy
confederations. The Shark Men's King
Kala is no friend of Emperor Ming and
his ally only reluctantly. He readily
gives Flash refuge, but later, in a change
of heart, locks him in a room (his
palace is like a spacious, endless
submarine) that fills with water and a
dread, tentacled Octosac. To Flash's

140

The turrets of the Shark Men's underwater city,

... has difficulties with King Kala's minions.

good fortune, Aura manages to save him by shutting off the water, but in their struggle against Kala the great pumps providing air to the undersea palace are stopped. Ming, watching on his televisor, uses huge magnets to bring the shark palace to the surface in order to save his daughter's life. Barely have our friends made their escape when Dale and Thun are captured by other examples of Mongo's racial oddities, the Hawk Men, winged creatures who carry them away to their sky city, which is kept suspended above the clouds by powerful atomic rays.

Here the serial's finest episodes follow. Flash has freed Zarkov, and the two are joined by another ally, Prince Barin, true ruler of Mongo, who was dethroned when Ming killed his father. The three steal a rocket and make their way to the sky city. Meanwhile, in the palace of the Hawk Men (the serial seems to proceed from one royal abode to another), Dale has made another conquest: bearded, boisterous King Vultan, with great feathery wings sprouting from his back, also wishes to marry her. True to form, he claps Zarkov into *his* laboratory. And, eyeing Flash's strength, he imprisons the Earthman and Barin in the atomic furnace rooms of the floating city, as slaves to feed radium to the power generator that keeps the city suspended.

The furnaces, row upon row of them stoked by chained and beaten prisoners, are operated by devices and controls showing heavy borrowings from the machinery of Fritz Lang's *Metropolis;* it is a singularly impressive scene. Tireless Flash, his muscular body glistening, hurls his electrically charged shovel into the furnace and succeeds in short-circuiting the entire city! Its power blacked out, the rays that keep it aloft dying, the sky city begins to lurch tipsily in space—and descend!

With marvelous foresight, however, Zarkov, still locked in Vultan's laboratory, has managed to invent an

alternative means of suspending the
city, and he switches it on. In gratitude,
Vultan releases Flash and his friends.
But Ming craftily cites an ancient
tradition to be fulfilled before Flash
can win his freedom: the Earthman
must battle a hooded gladiator, the
greatest swordsman on Mongo, and the
winner can claim the bride of his
choice. Flash handily bests his
opponent and, removing the hood,
discovers it is his friend Prince Barin,
whom Ming has gotten to turn on Flash
through some dark, unexplained
trickery. Enraged and completely
unsportsmanlike, Ming releases a great
horned "orangopoid" ape into the
arena, where Flash still is. Aura
manages to inform Flash that its horn is
the beast's vulnerable spot, and he
scores his second victory.

Ming can hardly withdraw his
gladiatorial prizes without losing face,

so with a flourish he declares three days
of feasting to commence, to be
climaxed by the wedding of Flash and
Dale—the *third* set of nuptial
arrangements made for the girl since
she landed on Mongo. This gives Ming
three more days to scheme. For Flash,
the next episodes are full of incident
very similar to the challenges in a
medieval saga: he is given a drug of
forgetfulness, and Aura plots with the
kingdom's high priest to make Flash
think he is to marry her instead (the
serial has as much talk of weddings as
the June issue of a women's magazine);
the industrious Zarkov then restores
Flash's memory and, using his newest
invention, makes him invisible to his
enemies.

This lasts for only a short time, and
Flash is soon back at his old battles:
the palace guards, Ming's soldiers, and
such exotic zoology as fire dragons and

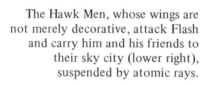

The Hawk Men, whose wings are not merely decorative, attack Flash and carry him and his friends to their sky city (lower right), suspended by atomic rays.

a maned species of tiger called "tigron." By chapter thirteen, the finale, two important decisions have been made: Princess Aura has decided love is possible for her only with another of her royal station, and she falls for Prince Barin; while Zarkov, "in the interests of science," decides to rocket his little party back home. (This was unlike the comic strip, which left Flash and his friends on Mongo for seven years, until a very compelling reason—World War II—caused them to visit Earth for a time.) They are free to leave Mongo because of the sudden and

A slave to the atomic furnaces that keep the sky city aloft, Flash labors tirelessly under the whips of the Hawk Men . . . and plots his escape.

somewhat inexplicable death of Ming:
he had unwisely wandered toward the
flaming pyres before the altar of the
Sacred Temple of the God Tao, while
outside the crematorium his high priest,
obviously deranged (he is cackling
wildly), seizes the opportunity to shut
the gates, thus sealing the emperor
inside. On a determined assassination
spree, the cleric also wires a time bomb
into the rocket ship, but Flash and
Zarkov easily defuse it on their
homeward trip. The journey is
uneventful except for its final
moments, when, hurtling over New
York City, Zarkov radios a plea that
the city's electricity be momentarily
switched off, so that there can be no
magnetic drain on his landing controls.
There is unhesitating response: the
lights of Manhattan go dark,
anticipating the first metropolitan
electrical blackout!

Inspired by *Flash Gordon's* success,
Universal issued a sequel two years
later. *Flash Gordon's Trip to Mars* is a
switch in location, but we soon
discover that the red planet is a series
of kingdoms much like Mongo and that
Ming has made himself quite at home
there. (There is no explanation of how

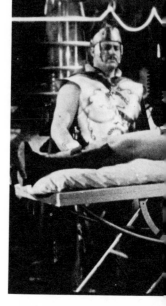

King Vultan of Sky City puts Flash to another
electrifying test (above), causing Prince Barin, Dr.
Zarkov, and Dale great concern (right). And in
his throne room Vultan welcomes his
monarch Ming and prepares to turn the
Earthman Flash over to him (far right).

he escaped death in the previous serial, but in the first chapter of this new effort he is given the opportunity to demonstrate that he can walk through fire. The alert viewer can conclude he is impervious to flame.) Ming has convinced Mars' Queen Azura to join him in his favorite occupation: destroying Earth. This time he uses a Nitron Lamp to bombard our planet with earthquakes and cyclones. Naturally Flash, Dale, and Zarkov blast off for Mars to shut off the Nitron Lamp.

Although its budget was less than its predecessor's, *Trip to Mars* offered some opulent visuals—the Martian cities are stunning backdrops of domes and light-bridges very much based on Alex Raymond's designs—and quite inventive situations: Queen Azura's political enemies, for instance, are transformed by her magical powers into living clay, creatures with clay bodies but lumpy human shapes, forced to remain like

some lost race of outcast gnomes in deep grottoes under the earth from which they cannot emerge. Flash eventually liberates the Clay People, restoring their humanity, in what many think is the most poetic and best of his three serials. (A feature version of this second chapterplay, completed but then shelved, was hastily released under the title *Mars Attacks the World* one week after Orson Welles's "Martian scare" radio show—despite the serial's far greater resemblance to a rich and almost medieval fantasy than to H. G. Wells's scientific tale of alien invasion.)

Even though when we last see him on Mars he is about to be disintegrated, two years later, in the third serial to

Flash and his party prepare to blast off for Earth in their sputtering rocket ship from Mongo's aptly named Valley of Despair.

chronicle Flash's adventures, Ming turns up back home on Mongo again, sneering his hatred of Earth and sending a spacefleet of plague ships to wipe out the human race. (Ming's plague, a discriminating Purple Death that strikes only at those with intelligence, and spares the dumb and the docile, would be the envy of any dictator out to subdue worlds.) Of course, Flash and his friends head for Mongo once more, and this time they have a chance to explore other regions of the planet: the northern wastes of glacial Frigia, and the lovely forest kingdom of pastoral Arboria. Flash tangles with an army of walking robot bombs called Annihilatons, finds and finally frees a degenerate race of Rock Men (a cousin species to the Clay People of Mars) living among the craters of the Land of the Dead, and suffers at the treachery of an Other Woman (Anne Gwenne as a blond, voluptuous Sonja).

At the end, Flash—parachuting out just in time—pilots a rocket into a tower where Ming is about to order the destruction of the Earth; the emperor supposedly perishes in the explosion. "There is only one way out of the tower," a minion chortles, "and Ming would probably not have thought of it!" (We know, with suspicious lines like that, that we are being set up for yet another sequel.) Zarkov turns to Flash and says with Euclidian logic, "Ming conquered the universe, and you have just conquered Ming. Therefore, Flash Gordon, you have conquered the universe!" The title of the third serial was *Flash Gordon Conquers the Universe*. And, really, where can you go from there?

Despite Ming's secret escape route from his tower, he never turned up again. There was to be no fourth serial. World War II was beginning, and battles here on Earth were taking precedence over tournaments on Mongo. The serials quickly achieved the status of

149

Ming, fatalistic in defeat, walks toward the flames of the Sacred Temple. . . .

warmly remembered nostalgia and represented the "finest moment" for nearly everyone in them, including Frank Shannon as Zarkov, Priscilla Lawson as a sexy Princess Aura, Richard Alexander as a beefy, loyal Prince Barin—actors who achieved perfection in their roles yet were hardly ever noticed in anything else again. The serials themselves seemed unduplicatable, one-of-a-kind: no others tried to imitate their special style, and a Flash Gordon television series filmed in Europe during the fifties was a soulless failure.

The very name "Flash Gordon"

today connotes innocence and naïveté rooted firmly in the past, a variety of space opera that contemporary science fiction will never explore again. Today's real astronauts—and tomorrow's—will never land on worlds where inhabitants dress—as sometimes did whole populations in the *Flash Gordon* films and comic strips—in Greek or Roman robes, or tights, or bright Graustarkian uniforms. And yet, perhaps they will. In the alternative universe that is the fantastic cinema, Apollo space probes may yet cross the clouds over Mongo's lofty palace spires.

THINGS TO COME

(The Shape of Things to Come)

John Cabal/Oswald Cabal	Raymond Massey
Pippa Passworthy/Raymond Passworthy	Edward Chapman
Rudolph	Ralph Richardson
Roxana	Margaretta Scott
Theotocopulos	Sir Cedric Hardwicke
Dr. Harding	Maurice Braddell
Mrs. John Cabal	Sophie Stewart
Richard Gordon	Derrick de Marney
Mary Gordon	Ann Todd
Catherine Cabal	Pearl Argyle
Maurice Passworthy	Kenneth Villiers
Morden Mitani	Ivan Brandt
The Child	Anne McLaren
The Airman	John Clements
Simon Burton	Anthony Holles
Grandfather Cabal	Alan Jeayes
Horrie Passworthy	Pickles Livingston
Janet Gordon	Patricia Hilliard

Directed by William Cameron Menzies
Produced by Alexander Korda
Scenario by Herbert George Wells, based on his *Shape of Things to Come*
Photography by George Perinal
Settings designed by Vincent Korda
Special effects directed by Ned Mann
Music composed by Arthur Bliss
Musical director: Muir Mathieson
Costumes designed by John Armstrong, René Hubert, the Marchioness of Queensberry
Aeronautical advice: Nigel Tangye

151

A London Films production
Released (in the United States)
April 24, 1936

Herbert George Wells, an English shopkeeper's son born in 1866, was the astonishing prophet of the twentieth century. He unfolded its wonders and horrors before the audiences of his day—peering eagerly out of their changing Victorian world—and led them with zest and ease into an imaginative world he confidently expected to be the coming Golden Age of Science, just around the corner. He was a journalist, philosopher, historian, political radical, and social reformer, but most memorably he was the exhilarating spokesman for things to come.

Already by 1900 he had predicted television, planes that flew over oceans, cars and superhighways, air-conditioning, moving sidewalks, and much else. By the end of the first decade of the twentieth century he had envisioned the armored-tank juggernauts of "modern" war, as well as air warfare, during which fleets of planes would obliterate cities; in 1913 he wrote seriously of an atomic bomb manufactured from uranium. Most of the breathlessly on-target "scientific romances" for which we remember him today—*The War of the Worlds, The Time Machine, The Invisible Man, The Island of Dr. Moreau*—were written before the turn of the century! His vision of the future was remarkable, and his faith in it total. He foresaw a utopia wrought by and ruled by science. Although he felt this coming social order was inevitable, he was determined to hasten and to smooth its arrival by frenzied writing and intellectual pamphleteering.

By the nineteen thirties Wells was an extraordinarily vigorous man in his sixties, still highly regarded as a thinker and as a man who had educated and electrified generations. Yet somehow Wells, whose zealous attempts to reform and ennoble the species were unflagging, had come to be regarded as a charming relic. He had, after all, been around a long time. His ability to detail in broad strokes the progress of civilizations had resulted in the publication, in the previous decade, of his mammoth and popular *Outline of History*. He had toyed with the idea of bringing the history up to date, but the idea bored him; he realized it would have little impact. Instead, he would sweep his new work of "history" beyond the present into an apocalyptic vision of future world events and would title it *The Shape of Things to Come.*

The book—one can hardly call it a novel, since it is more a philosophic inquiry into the possibilities of the future—appeared in 1933. Wells's device is a manuscript outline of a history of the future, which, set down as it had come to him in a dream, is found in the effects of a dead League of Nations official.

The dream had some surprisingly accurate prophetic shots. World war breaks out in 1940. It starts as a conflict over Poland, igniting Germany, Italy, and the Balkan states. It is a war fought in the air, with radio-controlled missile torpedoes leveling cities; however (as was not to be the case) all nations make extensive use of poison gases. Eventually, battered by wave after wave of war, civilization crumbles. Pestilence reduces great cities to villages, and all communication between places ends. Petty leaders arise, whipping their village packs into acts of barbarism. But there remain a few planes, the only machines still capable of uniting the fragments of the crumbled world, and it is the young airmen and the remaining young technicians and scientists who with typical Wellsian flourish take charge of things, sweep away the rubble, and build the model "Modern State." Wells's faith in science was undiminished.

Despite being a book of philosophic and social speculation, *The Shape of Things to Come*, envigorated by the vitality of Wells's style, became a best seller. It was, of course, considered wild sensationalism, and no one took its author's very specific predictions about the coming importance of Hitler and the possibilities of a second world war at all seriously. Wells was indulgently regarded as an amusing intellectual, outmoded, but with a certain amount of tradition and prestige linked to him. It was the prestige that interested Alexander Korda.

After a short time spent at American film studios, the great Hungarian film producer found Hollywood too encrusted with nepotism and rigid systems to suit him and so moved to Britain, where he was already revolutionizing that country's less developed film industry. With *The Private Life of Henry VIII* he brought British films to international attention—and markets. Already in the planning stages were such important productions as *Catherine the Great* and *The Scarlet Pimpernel.* Korda saw Wells's scientific prophecy as a prestige film with world appeal, and he approached the author with the suggestion that he do a screenplay of it under the more specifically futuristic title *One Hundred Years to Come.* (This was later abandoned for the simpler *Things to Come*.) Wells, challenged and intrigued, agreed—committing himself to the task by signing the back of a postcard.

Wells threw himself into every aspect of the production. He dictated all the moods of the film's music—bringing it into "the constructive scheme of the film"—and rightly praised Arthur Bliss's "admirable" compositions. He admonished his cast (by memo) that the populace of his future cities would not live like the mindless automatons of UFA's *Metropolis*, slaves to the machine, but would actually be freed by automatic machines from mundane tasks in order to pursue their own pleasures—no doubt a far more accurate picture of work and leisure in the next century. Wells even designed the film's futuristic costumes: simple tunic and cloak affairs—as he requested, *no* "costumes of cellophane illuminated by neon"—with wide padded shoulders to stand in place of pockets, for carrying wallets and pens and the like, and the suggestion of floor-length dress for the ladies, since there would be no dirt to muss them up in the hygienic new world. Happily, less skirt with more leg was decided on for the film itself. And interestingly enough, Wells clearly anticipates a world of ever-present transistor radios.

While Wells had no difficulty in imagining the wonders to come, he had great trouble in fashioning a screenplay. It soon became apparent that the plotless speculations of his philosophic book could in no way be translated into a workable feature film. The first treatment was discarded; a second treatment was completely rewritten. Wells added new characters to every decade of his future history and linked this future to three generations of a single family of heroic leaders called Cabal: the "living embodiment of the spirit of human adventure."

Attempting to help Wells in his unsteady labors (Wells had only once before tried his hand at a screen scenario, an impractical allegory that was never filmed) was the Hungarian writer Lajos Biro, who had written many of Korda's most successful motion pictures, including *The Private Life of Henry VIII*, and in whom Korda had a great deal of trust.

Also assisting Wells in visualizing his

future world was the man Korda imported to direct *Things to Come*, the brilliant American designer William Cameron Menzies. Menzies, together with special-effects director Ned Mann and settings designer Vincent Korda, created the fantastic Everytown (actually a London composite including Oxford Circus and the dome of Saint Paul's), which evolves from a contemporary bustling city to one devastated by war, a ravished Dark Age ruin, and finally a futuristic metropolis, symbol of a new civilization. Brilliant special-effects work either utilized elaborate miniatures or mixed—by means of a split-screen process—actual lower structures of buildings and streets, with people moving through them, and miniatures of the upper structures towering skyward. Motion pictures of moving crowds projected against tiny screens set up within complex miniatures—or crowds of tiny "people" moving on tracks across mini-streets—gave an illusion of realism to panoramas of the cities of the future.

Unfortunately Menzies was far more at home with the technical aspects of screen design, with the look of things, than he was with people. He was uncomfortable directing actors and was unable to prevent Wells's creations from becoming street-corner orators—in rich voice, but living pamphets all the same. Happily the highly visual spectacle that Menzies created so well did much to compensate for the flatness of the film's characters, whom Wells insisted were not so much people as symbols of stages in a changing civilization.

Symbols or not, the actors chosen by Korda for *Things to Come* were from his own special group of talented stock players, with solid backgrounds in the British stage: fairly obscure performers who were all later to become international stars. Canadian-born

Raymond Massey had already (in 1931) played Sherlock Holmes, and had been in a number of Korda vehicles. Playing several generations of the heroic Cabals, who lead the world out of war's aftermath, he gives us more than a hint, in strength, if not in accent, of his famous later portrayal of Abraham Lincoln.

Ralph Richardson, who had previously done several screen melodramas including *The Return of Bulldog Drummond*, was a vigorous Rudolph, the Boss. Ernest Thesiger had been tested for the role of Theotocopulos, the artisan who rebels against progress, but he had left for America, and the somewhat meatier role of Dr. Praetorius in *The Bride of Frankenstein*. He was replaced by Cedric Hardwicke.

As the shooting progressed at Korda's old London Studios—the construction of his new, modern Denham Studios was just being completed, and this was the last of his epics to be filmed at the former location—Wells visited the set daily, sometimes pleased, sometimes storming that the cinema had limited his own epic vision. (Involving himself in everything, he even complained that the filming was taking too long and was wasteful.) When the film finally appeared, his name was all over the posters, printed across vistas of a splendid, futuristic world, a world we see only in the final third of the motion picture, a world so antiseptic (Wells insisted it be dirt-free) and luxurious that nothing ever happens except for a moon flight that most people are too complacent to be interested in. How prophetic Wells was here! The philosophic intrusions and the bloodless, zestless style of life presented in this final third of the film made *Things to Come* unsatisfying to many people. Prophecy was an uncomfortable sport, in the thirties at

154

any rate, and elderly prophets tended to be ignored. It took several years for *Things to Come* to recoup its investment; people dismissed its predictions of war and were only faintly stirred by its future marvels. In the long run, though, *Things to Come* is a unique film of its kind: an unduplicated blueprint of the next hundred years, of world chaos and world recovery. Its vision of and concern for humanity are staggering, and its philosophic dialogues, while impeding drama, provoke the mind. It is both an intelligent and a spectacular contribution to the cinema of the fantastic.

Its very opening strives to convey its epic scope: a searchlight plays against the letters *Things to Come*, giant against the horizon. Immediately the audience is catapulted four years forward to 1940: it is Christmas in the bustling London-like city called Everytown. Carolers sing, shops burst with toys, but, in counterpoint, newspaper headlines warn of war: EUROPE ARMING, WAR STORM BREWING, STRAITS DISPUTE ACUTE. The conflict seems far removed, however, from the comfortable suburban home of John Cabal, an airplane engineer. The first guest of his Christmas party arrives, young Dr. Harding. They talk of the war rumors, which Harding refuses to take seriously; the papers are all crying wolf. "Some day the wolf will come," muses Cabal. His portly neighbor Passworthy dismisses it all with a laugh. "Threatened men live long; threatened wars don't occur."

The families proceed to open presents under the tree—there are a good many toy soldiers and cannons for the children—when suddenly artillery is heard in the distance. And heavy artillery. Over the radio comes an announcement: "Orders for a general

mobilization have been issued and the precautionary civilian organization against gas will at once be put into operation." War has come at last! Passworthy is indignant: "If they've attacked without a declaration of war—then it's vengeance! No quarter!"

The whole of Everytown mobilizes against attack. Tanks and trucks roar through the central square; loudspeakers warn against air raids, and frightened mobs grab at gas masks and scurry for the shelter of the subway entrances. Then the bombs come. The city square is obliterated by explosions; the antiaircraft fire is helpless. Destruction and death are everywhere, in a remarkable foretelling of just what did happen in the London war bombings only a few years later. Column after column of soldiers march off to war, moving into a shadowland from which we know they will not return. A small boy in soldier's cap—Passworthy's son—beats a toy drum as he tramps up and down his suburban lane. Behind him in the mists shadow armies loom and march. They march to their death, as does the boy, who is killed by a bomb.

Great armadas of planes dogfight across the skies. Fighter pilot John Cabal brings down an enemy aircraft and follows it to the ground. The enemy pilot has already crawled from his burning machine, from which dark clouds of gas rise ominously. Cabal looks at the badly wounded young flier and groans, "Why should we be murdering each other?" But the other warns him to escape, since the gas from his plane is poisonous. Cabal dons his mask and helps the pilot put on his. Suddenly a small girl runs up, bewildered, and the pilot removes his own gas mask to hand it to her. "I've given plenty of the gas to others," he says, coughing. "Why shouldn't I have a whiff myself?" All Cabal can do is hand his gun to the airman. As he moves to

155

his plane, he hears more coughing—and a shot.

Tanks cross a world scarred with trenches. The fighting is endless. Years pass. By 1970 Everytown is a crumbled ruin and its remaining inhabitants have retreated to near barbarism. In the wake of the conflict and the subsequent breakdown of civilization a strange pestilence has spread throughout the world: the Wandering Sickness. Mindless, capable of transmitting a virulent infection, its victims move through streets and fields until they topple. Even more deadly than the Black Death of the Middle Ages, the Wandering Sickness kills more than half the human race. No one who catches it survives. It also provides the means for brutal leaders to rise to power: the swaggering, aggressive Rudolph has mobilized a militia to shoot all Wandering Sickness carriers on sight. Gradually the pestilence is eliminated and Everytown begins to function as a community again—still at war with the enemy outside its boundaries, "the hill people," and still primitive, for no industry remains. Human life has degenerated to senseless territorial squabbles, and Everytown is marshaled under the iron-fisted rule of Rudolph, the "Boss," jaunty in his

military tunic, coat of animal fur, and air warden's helmet.

Dr. Harding, the young doctor who attended the Christmas party in the opening scene, is now middle-aged and haggard and, without his medical supplies, helpless to treat the sick. His daughter Mary's husband, Richard Gordon, a former airplane technician who is now Master Mechanic to the Boss, also deplores his lack of tools: "Nothing will ever fly again. Flying is over." Mary seems to think she heard an airplane pass overhead at dawn: clearly an impossible notion.

Herbert George Wells, largely overlooked today but a strikingly popular philosopher of the early decades of this century, explains some of the intricacies of his script to his players. Below, a view of Everytown; at upper left, a part of the set for the city after the holocaust of war.

157

Everytown on the brink of war.
The headlines are grim, and
platoons of soldiers roar through
the city streets. Concerned citizens
such as engineer John Cabal and his
wife (below) fear the worst. And
the worst does come. The war is
fought on the ground with
explosives and poison gases (lower
left) and in the air as well.

Rudolph is furious with Gordon for
not providing him with planes with
which to counterattack against the hill
people. The Boss's calculating mistress,
Roxana, gives Gordon an imperious
look while taunting her lover: "I
thought you could make anybody do
anything." Suddenly the sound of an
engine is heard in the sky. The entire
population of Everytown cranes to gaze
upward, incredulous. A gleaming,
futuristic craft, aerodynamically
curved, glides across the sky. A *new*
machine, Gordon gasps. Somewhere
they are still making them! The plane
circles, to land outside the town.
Rudolph, his ego bruised by the
thought that someone has planes while
he has none, demands that the plane's
occupant be arrested and brought at
once to him.

The airplane is small, compact, a
single-seater. Out of it—gray-haired but
still young-looking and dressed in a
dramatic, severe black uniform with a
huge, domed, transparent helmet—steps
John Cabal. He has been away from
Everytown a long time, and the
decadence following the war seems not
to have touched him. The oafish militia
arrest him, which Cabal accepts with a
superior grace: he wants to see their
Boss, and that is where they are taking
him.

On the way Cabal recognizes his old
friend Harding and pauses at his
primitive hospital for a chat, to the
chagrin of his guards. He explains to
Harding and his daughter and
son-in-law that he and all who are left
of the old engineers and mechanics are
working toward salvaging the world.
"The freemasonry of efficiency. The
brotherhood of science. We are the
trustees of civilization when all else has
failed." It is what Gordon has been
waiting for all his life. "I'm yours to
command," he cries, but Cabal puts up
his hand. "Not mine. No more bosses.
Civilization's to command."

159

More of Rudolph's guards come, and Cabal good-naturedly lets himself be taken to the Boss's office in Everytown's City Hall, where sunlight streams through a smashed domed roof. Rudolph, ever shrewd and aggressive, realizes that his extraordinary visitor is a prize and must be dealt with cautiously. Cabal stands easy. He identifies himself: he represents law and sanity, and his group of airmen, who call themselves Wings over the World, rule themselves under a government of common sense.

Rudolph cannot grasp this. His is an independent, combative state that is at war; he needs planes and fuel, and his visitor obviously has both. Cabal makes it clear that his group approves of neither independent, combative states nor warfare, and that they intend to stop them. His group, headquartered on the Mediterranean, is slowly restoring order, trade, and industry throughout the area. They have hundreds of planes and are making more. And if Cabal doesn't return soon, they will send a force out after him.

Rudolph, ruffled by this threat, roars, "They'll find me ready! Take this man away! If he gives any trouble, *club* him! Did you hear that, Mr. Wings over your Wits?" And Cabal is escorted to a detention room below.

In the next days Rudolph's forces score a victory over the hill people, and a supply of crude oil is captured from the ancient hill refineries. Gordon is expected to convert the oil into aviation fuel to power whatever planes he can bring into the air again. He asks for the assistance of both Harding and the prisoner Cabal, the first because of his knowledge of chemistry to adapt the oil, the second because of his knowledge of engines. Rudolph reluctantly gives permission, after Roxana informs him that he is really bullying people too hard.

On the night of the victory there is a

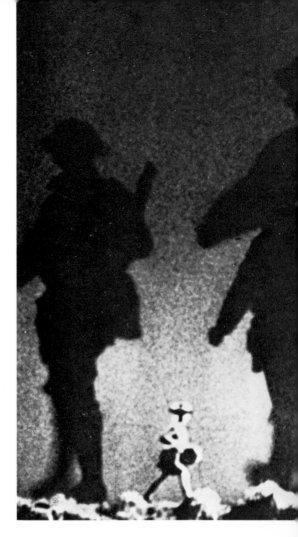

wild celebration—with the Boss at his swaggering best. "Some people complain there are no more cinemas! There's no more travel! Well, what do we need *travel* for? Isn't our land good enough?" Roxana slips away to visit Cabal in his cell. He is the most interesting thing to happen to Everytown in years, she tells him. His talk of the Mediterranean, of communes and factories, makes her realize once again there is a great world outside. She is not stupid; unlike the other young people she learned to read before education stopped, and while she adores Rudolph, his strength and his firmness, and while she has all the luxury to be had here, she knows life in Everytown is *limited*. . . .

Passworthy's young son thrills to the adventure of soldiering—as shadowy armies march by him to doom (left). The carnage is immense.

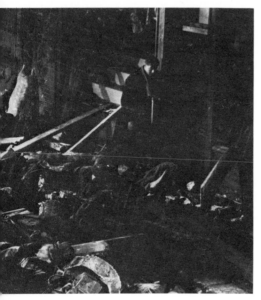

Rudolph bursts upon them both.
Roxana, pretending she has been
interrogating Cabal, urges Rudolph to
make peace with the airman and let
him go. Rudolph, who has been
drinking heavily, refuses. "There's no
making peace between you and me," he
says to Cabal. "It's your world or
mine—and it's going to be *mine!*"

The next day Richard Gordon
manages to lift one of his antique
planes into the air, and he heads for the
Mediterranean headquarters of Wings
over the World. It is a splendidly
futuristic airfield and cluster of
buildings; on runways beyond sit planes
so immense they would dwarf even the
jumbo jets of today. Crewmen,
appearing tiny as ants, board monstrous
aircraft with incredible wingspreads.
Gordon is overwhelmed, but he
manages to blurt out his story to
Cabal's fellow airmen. A rescue mission
is formed immediately. "And we'll get
a chance to use the Peace Gas!"

The massive airships of Wings over

the World loom in the skies above
Everytown. Rudolph and his men have
anticipated an invasion—they have kept
Cabal ready as hostage—but the
incredible power of the air armada
above them drives them into panic and
terror. There is no defense; everyone
runs helplessly for shelter as gas bombs
explode across the square. The first of
hundreds of parachutists, all wearing
the same severe black uniform as
Cabal's, have landed. Only Rudolph
offers any sort of resistance, shooting
his pistol aimlessly and screaming at the
heavens. Finally a peace gas bomb
bursts near him and he collapses. Later,
when all revive from the tranquilizing
effects of the gas, they, curiously
enough, find Rudolph dead. "And his
world dead with him," intones Cabal.
The Boss could not or would not
outlast his reign. "Now for the rule of
the airmen and a new life for
mankind."

It is only one small victory for the
rule of science. Other brigand chiefs

By 1970 Everytown—ravaged by war and by
the Wandering Sickness—has been reduced to
near barbarism. But a plane is heard overhead.
An aviator lands!

elsewhere and all vestiges of war must
be dealt with before the process of
rebuilding society can properly begin.
As Cabal sketches his dream of the
future for his fellow airmen, he knows
none will see their new world
finished—but their children will. A time
of furious activity begins. First,
excavation. Gigantic machines dig deep
below the surface of the earth,
scooping out its metals, creating valleys
where none existed. Then more
sophisticated machines replace the
excavators, multileveled machines
spawning multileveled machines, an age
of technocracy and unending circuits,
of power plants larger than cities, of
goliath machinery before which
humans move merely incidental and
supervisory.

Finally it is the year 2036 (a date
one hundred years after the making of
the film) and Everytown is an airy,
roomy metropolis *under the ground,*
under the landscaped walks and hills of
the surface world where the old city

once stood in ruins. The camera swoops down beneath a vast circular opening to a great square of many-tiered dwellings, terraces reaching as far as the eye can see, trees and shrubs and ramps and elevators shooting up transparent tubular shafts. There is always "sunlight"—in direct contrast to the sunless underground hovels of *Metropolis*—and the air is so pure that respiratory diseases belong to the past. Even though there is a feeling of vast openness about Everytown, the streets and levels are full of people. But the people are promenading, for this is an age of leisure.

Oswald Cabal, grandson of John Cabal, sits as president of the council in this brave new world, this triumph of human invention and will over nature, but his restless, energetic blood rebels against Everytown's comfort and security. His mind is on the conquest of the moon. (Wells's timetable of prophecy was well off here, since we actually stepped onto the moon's surface more than six decades earlier than he predicted.) Already a Space Gun had been constructed, its base sunk into the cliffs outside Everytown. The base of the vertical Gun, embedded deep in concrete, was a series of chambers fitted within chambers (the design was that of German rocket expert Willy Ley) capable of firing in sequence and sending a projectile beyond the pull of earth's gravity and around the moon. But who will be the two young people selected to man this rocket?

Thousands have applied for the chance, but Maurice Passworthy, the blond, handsome son of Oswald Cabal's friend Raymond, and grandson of John Cabal's old friend, begs to be chosen. "You ought not to send two people you do not know. It was her idea even more than it is mine." *Her* idea? Young Passworthy blurts out that he wants for his copilot Cabal's eighteen-year-old

John Cabal of Wings over the World remains calm while interrogated by a suspicious Rudolph, "Boss" of this savage new world (left). For Roxana, Rudolph's mistress, the aviator is the most interesting thing to happen to Everytown in years (lower left). Cabal has a chance to inspect Gordon's ancient planes (below).

Gordon says
good-bye to his
wife and joins
Wings over the
World at their
Mediterranean base
(center). Rudolph
exhorts his
squadron to war
(below) but is no
match for the
armada in the
clouds.

daughter, Catherine. Cabal is stunned for a moment. But then he sees he can do little but consent.

Yet there is apprehension in the squares of Everytown; not everybody approves of the new age into which the firing of the Space Gun will bring humanity. The rebel artisan Theotocopulos has been granted permission to express his views over the public television system. His image is projected onto an immense transparent screen over the great square and onto thousands of other receivers throughout the city. "An end to Progress! An end to journeying to strange planets and abominable places beyond the stars! Let this be the last day of the Scientific Age! Make this Space Gun the symbol of all that drives us, and destroy it—now!" Many in Everytown agree with him. The populace is aroused, and in an ugly mood.

Young Maurice's father, Raymond Passworthy, is not enthusiastic about his son's volunteering. He turns to Cabal in anguish. "Why do you let your daughter dream of going on this mad moon journey?" But Cabal is as much a visionary as his forebears. He is letting his daughter go because he loves her. He wants her to live Life to the fullest. There is no happiness in mere contentment. The new world did not abolish death and danger; it made them worthwhile. At that moment a young council member bursts upon them. "The Space Gun is in urgent danger! It's a race against time to save it. A crowd of people are heading for it; they're going to break it up. They say it's a symbol of your tyranny." The Peace Gas could stop the mob, but not enough of it is ready at hand. However, the Gun is primed for lift-off and, if fired within the next two hours, can still reach the moon.

A trim white helicopter takes the young people and their fathers to the Gun, a massive metallic structure rising above an open plain overlooking the

sea. The mob has not yet reached it, and it is deserted. The youngsters quickly enter and are strapped down inside a slim projectile, which is raised high by pulley and lowered inside the mouth of the Space Gun. The mob appears, but it already is too late. Theotocopulos shouts out to Cabal, "We want to put an end to this foolery. Your science and inventions are everlastingly changing life for us . . . making what we think great, seem small, what we think strong seem feeble! We don't want you in the same world! We shall hate you more if you succeed than if you fail! Destroy the Gun!" But, even though the mob spills over the gun's cradle and outer ramps, it is already in firing position. "Beware the concussion," Cabal warns. There is an ear-shattering explosion, with great clouds of smoke. . . .

In an observatory, Cabal and Passworthy look into a vast reflection of the starry heavens, across which the projectile bearing their children is a speck moving steadily toward the circle

Rudolph rings the alarm. Firing his pistol into the air and shouting commands, he is belligerent to the end (far left). But his world is finished. The peace gas overcomes everyone; for Rudolph it is fatal (left). John Cabal walks through the square as the dazed inhabitants begin to stir. "Now for the rule of the airmen. . . ."

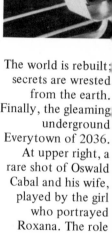

The world is rebuilt;
secrets are wrested
from the earth.
Finally, the gleaming
underground
Everytown of 2036.
At upper right, a
rare shot of Oswald
Cabal and his wife,
played by the girl
who portrayed
Roxana. The role
was later dropped.

of the moon. Cabal is stirred with
emotion: the moon will be conquered
and the planets about us, and then
finally the immensity of the stars. And
even when Man has conquered all the
deeps of space and the mysteries of
time, still he will only be beginning his
voyage of discovery. Passworthy,
anxious and afraid, retorts, "Is there
never to be an age of happiness? Is
there never to be any rest?" Rest
enough for the individual; too much
and too soon: death. But for *Man,* no
rest and no ending. *He must go on.*

But we are such fragile creatures,
Passworthy pleads, like "little animals."

In H. G. Wells's finest cinematic
moment, as Arthur Bliss's music soars

170

and swells in the background, Cabal turns to his friend: "If we are no more than animals, we must snatch our little scraps of happiness and live and suffer and pass, mattering no more than all the animals do or have done. Is it that—or this? *All the universe*—or nothingness? Which shall it be? Which shall it be?" A chorus of massed voices picks up the question as the camera sweeps beyond Cabal's impassioned face to the immensity of the galaxies.

Alexander Korda, confident that *Things to Come* would be a critical success, immediately talked Wells into another project. Wells, far less certain of his grasp of the medium, chose for his next adaptation a work that was the opposite extreme of the epic he had just finished: a very brief, almost one-joke short story, "The Man Who Could Work Miracles," in which an ordinary young store clerk (played by Roland Young) is given by whim of the gods unlimited magical power. Naturally there is a good deal of philosophic discussion on everyone's part before the hero, having brought the whole world to the brink of destruction, wishes everything back the way it was before he acquired his miraculous powers. The film was heavy and overblown, and it did not make money. It was the last time Wells wrote for the screen, although he was to live until 1946, a bitter invalid disillusioned with a world that no longer paid him much attention.

As a matter of fact, others than Wells always fared better with his material. Several years before *Things to Come,* Hollywood had already produced a zesty yet faithful version of *The Invisible Man* (1933), directed by James Whale, and had brought *The Island of Dr. Moreau* to the screen as *Island of Lost Souls* (1933), with Charles Laughton as the vivisectionist surgeon. In 1938 an innovative young man

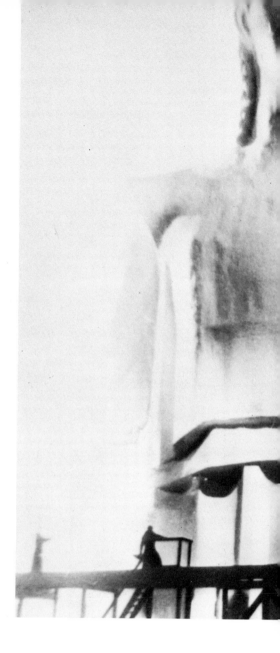

named Orson Welles took the turn-of-the-century *War of the Worlds,* stripped it of all philosophy, transplanted it to America, and mounted a Halloween radio broadcast that terrified the listening nation. Fifteen years later, film producer George Pal brought the same Wells novel to the screen and with a blood-chilling parade of exploding miniatures and special effects made

172

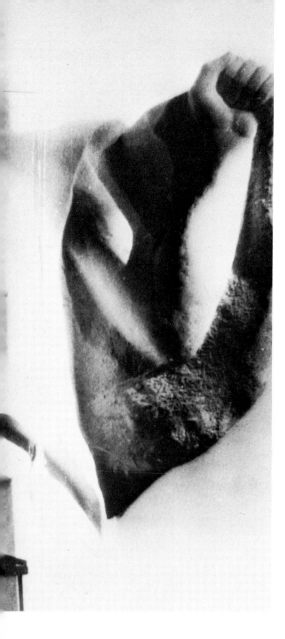

The rebel artist Theotocopulos (it is his sculpture above) addresses Everytown on public television (right): "An end to Progress! Destroy the Space Gun!" And some attempt it, by climbing the gun's superstructure (lower right).

The two young passengers of the Space Gun
are lowered inside it (above).
From an observatory, Cabal and Passworthy watch the flight.

"Which shall it be, Passworthy?" cries Cabal emotionally. "All the universe—or nothingness? Which shall it be?"

frighteningly real the author's vision of interplanetary invasion.

In 1960 Pal turned once more to Wells, fashioning of his *Time Machine* a poignant and haunting narrative of a Victorian inventor's journey (astride a machine bearing the maker's nameplate: Herbert George Wells) into the limitless future. And Ray Harryhausen's *First Men in the Moon* (1964) proved yet again how frequently up-to-the-minute Wells was. No doubt there are still more screen adaptations of Wells's stories ahead of us—a version of *When the Sleeper Wakes* has now been finished—for no other author aside from Verne has

contributed so many and so varying scientific romances to the screen.

And yet, despite the richness of Wells's contributions to the fantastic cinema, *Things to Come* stands unique. No other film has been made that quite attempts its chronology, or provides in such stirring detail the sweep of its hundred-year look into the future. Even though its heroes are somewhat cardboard and its brave new world somewhat placid, *Things to Come*'s singular vision makes it a film still very viewable today . . . and perhaps a film not too far out of date even when we catch up with it in the year 2036.

176

THE THIEF OF BAGDAD

Jaffar	Conrad Veidt
Abu	Sabu
Princess	June Duprez
Ahmad	John Justin
Djinni	Rex Ingram
Sultan	Miles Malleson
The Old King	Morton Selten
Halima	Mary Morris
The Merchant	Bruce Winston
Astrologer	Hay Petrie
Singer	Adelaide Hall
Jailer	Roy Emerton
The Story-Teller	Allan Jeayes

Produced by Alexander Korda
Associate Producers: Zoltan Korda, William Cameron Menzies
Production designed in color by Vincent Korda
Screenplay and dialogue: Miles Malleson
Scenario: Lajos Biro
Directed by: Ludwig Berger, Michael Powell, Tim Whelan
Special effects directed by Lawrence Butler
Photography: George Perinal and Osmond Borrodaile
Costumes designed by Oliver Messel, John Armstrong, Marcel Vertes
Musical score and songs: Miklos Rozsa
Musical director: Muir Mathieson
Supervising editor: William Hornbeck
A London Films production

Released (in the United States) December 25, 1940

Young Abu the thief, resisting mightily, is cast into prison, where he will meet Ahmad the king, also a prisoner. Together they will escape to Basra and high adventure.

It was an oriental fantasy—indeed, subtitled as such; pages snatched from the *Thousand and One Nights*. It was a fable of childhood, and its title role was played by a sixteen-year-old boy; yet it was an adventure for all ages, and for every age. It had breathtaking visual beauty and poetry enough to stir the soul; it was lavish as a jeweled palace in some secret scented Eastern valley. In the cinema of the fantastic it rates a special place, for it is quite unequaled. No other Arabian Nights extravaganza

has been able to match its wonders piled on wonders, its soaring majesty, its magic, its visions, its delights.

Only one other film even came close, and that was the motion picture on which it was based. The silent parent *Thief of Bagdad* was a Douglas Fairbanks, Sr., production of 1924, an opulent spectacle displaying the dashing, athletic Fairbanks as an engaging thief in ancient Bagdad, somewhat reformed by his love for the caliph's daughter, whose heart he seeks to win. In order to claim her he learns from a wise man that he must be courageous enough to find and possess a certain magic chest, and he does so after some fantastic adventures, returning to Bagdad just in time to save the kingdom of the caliph from the invading hordes of a Mongol prince.

Critics were unstinting in their praise for the film, calling the Bagdad of Fairbanks' creation "huge and dreamy, magnificent and imposing, lavish and wonderful; its splendor almost indescribable—outrivalling everything that has ever been attempted here or abroad." Fairbanks, who had already tackled Zorro and Robin Hood, continued with such examples of combined athletic zest and spectacle as *The Black Pirate* (1926) and *Mr. Robinson Crusoe* (1932). By the mid-thirties the increasing corpulence of middle age decided his retirement.

But let us jump ahead more than a decade from the original silent *Thief of Bagdad* . . . a Fairbanksian jump to

1938. The great Hungarian producer-director Alexander Korda, who had in this decade been hailed as the savior of the British film industry, had only the year previously produced in India a Rudyard Kipling story of hunting in the jungle, *Elephant Boy,* directed very naturalistically by Robert Flaherty with a largely native cast. The title role was played by a young Mysore stable boy discovered by Flaherty, and the film propelled the lad, Sabu, to instant stardom. Korda then quickly cast Sabu in a lavish color production of an A. E. W. Mason story about a young Indian prince who has learned army drum signals from a British drummer boy pal and manages to use these signals to warn the British regiment of a treacherous attack. *The Drum* was an enormous success both in England and in America (where it was called *Drums*), but Korda wanted to expand Sabu's usefulness by moving away from Kiplingesque themes. What would be more natural for the Indian teen-ager

than the eye-popping wonders of the Arabian Nights?

Inspiration sometimes strikes at unusual moments. At a banquet at London's Savoy Hotel following the premiere of *Drums,* Korda was seated across from Douglas Fairbanks, when he suddenly realized he would remake *The Thief of Bagdad,* utilizing an entirely new story and scaling down the title role—in size, not in vitality—for Sabu. The romantic interest would be provided by an exiled young king whom the boy thief aids with his wits and his skill at stealing. Could Korda buy the rights to the title, which Fairbanks owned? The latter agreed. Korda spent the next two years constructing an epic fantasy.

Korda felt strongly that world audiences would react against the grimness and uncertainty of the thirties by turning to themes of romance and escape. "When motion pictures became 'talkies,' " he said, "the world's greatest medium of entertainment suffered a tragic loss. Sound came in with a roar, and the imaginative beauty of the screen, with its unlimited magic sweep of movement, died out. Since the 'talkies' came, fantasy has been virtually unknown on the screen. The Walt Disney cartoons have kept it alive almost alone. In the excitement over Disney's successes, most of us forgot that he was teaching us a lesson." The lesson was not lost on Korda. He and his staff worked for two years at his Denham Studios outside London, creating the city of Bagdad and the

The sultan of Basra allows no one to set eyes on his only—and very beautiful—daughter. Before the princess rides by, the streets are cleared by an advance guard of horsemen and archers.

180

busy seaport of Basra in all their glory—temples, palaces, gardens, marketplaces, harbors, galleons—oriental settings of rich, colorful enchantment gorgeous enough to rival any Disney studio animation.

Korda was equally fortunate in his choice of cast. He selected John Justin and June Duprez as dashing lover and fragile princess. Black actor Rex Ingram, who had made a great impression as De Lawd in *Green Pastures* (1936) and the runaway slave Jim in *Huckleberry Finn* (1939), was to play the wildest role of his career as the djinni who billows out of a bottle. And as the villain Korda chose Conrad Veidt, the distinguished German player, who brought to his role of the evil grand vizier all of the dark sinister intensity of his great days at the height of UFA's expressionist terror cinema, where he played Dr. Caligari's somnambulist, history's legendary mesmerist Count von Cagliostro, and Orlac in the first version of *Mad Love*. A political exile from Germany, Veidt brought to his portrayal of Jaffar a demoniac force of such strength that one might well believe he could conjure up black spells and storms at sea. He was superb, a dramatic presence that lingers long in the memory.

The screenplay—unusually good, even poetic, and one of the very best examples of fantasy put into words—was the work of the delightful Miles Malleson, who, primarily an actor, for decades played a series of lovable old eccentrics (he was the doddering old sultan in this film). He died only recently. *The Thief of Bagdad* had three directors during the two years of its making; one of them was Michael Powell, already known as an extremely talented creator, who was to go on to direct many more imaginative and even bizarre films, from *The Red Shoes* (1948) to *Peeping Tom* (1962). A Hungarian (as was

181

The princess discovers what she thinks is a djinni at the bottom of her pool. "For me there can be no more beauty in the world, but yours," he declares. At right, the evil Jaffar steals the princess away: "I have powers that can force you to my will. . . ."

Korda), Miklos Rozsa, wrote the music for the film, lush and fantastic, often barbaric and with a touch of the Orient, but always sweeping and resplendent, underscoring the magic of the film itself.

Certainly a major contribution to the film was the work of special-effects genius William Cameron Menzies, an American who had already demonstrated his art in *Things to Come.* Curiously enough, while still in his twenties, Menzies had done the memorable designs for the original silent *Thief of Bagdad.* In the early 1930s he codirected *Chandu the Magician*—based on the popular radio plays and starring Edmund Lowe in the title role and Bela Lugosi as the villainous Luxor—in which, because much of it was set in exotic Arabian locales, Menzies was able to experiment with lesser versions of the effects he would use for Korda. As well, he was responsible for much of the epic sweep of *Gone With the Wind* (1939). Menzies was associate producer of the new *Thief of Bagdad,* along with Alexander's brother Zoltan Korda, while brother Vincent was production designer. The visuals in the film were lavish—and difficult, doubly so because of the use of color; that these visuals were brilliant testifies to the greatness of Vincent Korda and, especially, William Cameron Menzies.

After two years of shooting the film at Denham Studios, World War II erupted in Europe. The picture was to have been completed in Africa, but world conditions made this impossible. So Korda moved the entire company to Hollywood and shot the sequences originally intended for North Africa in the Painted Desert and the Grand Canyon, at Hopi Point and along the Colorado River.

Much else in the film also had to be reshot in Hollywood, and many of the massive Denham Studios sets rebuilt,

Jaffar demonstrates to the doddering old sultan his flying mechanical horse—demonstrating to *us* the breathtaking scope of this film's artistry and effects.

for young Sabu had grown alarmingly during the two years the film was being made. Sabu had started the epic as a boy, but had now filled out to young manhood, and the early scenes simply had to be redone.

The Thief of Bagdad begins in that turbulent ancient city, where a princess lies ill beyond recovery and where a handsome young beggar, sightless and guided by a mongrel dog, tells this strange tale: there was once a king, son of a king and a hundred kings, his subjects and his wealth uncountable, his power absolute. And the mongrel was not a dog but a little thief. . . .

The thief is young Abu, light-fingered and laughing, who finds it no hardship to live by his wits, leaping joyously across the rooftops of the city. The king is Ahmad, lonely and purposeless, for always his Grand Vizier Jaffar stands between him and his people. One night he determines to move among them as a commoner. In the streets and great squares, he hears prophecies of a liberator: "And this shall be the sign of him: he shall be the lowest of the low, and you shall look for him in the clouds." What is the name of the tyrant from whom the people cry for liberation? It is Ahmad. Himself. He hurries back to his palace and Jaffar, only to be thrown into prison as a madman, to be beheaded at dawn. Jaffar is the new king.

That night, in prison, Ahmad meets his first true friend—the little thief of Bagdad. Nimble of fingers, Abu steals the cell key from the warder, and he and Ahmad make for a small boat drifting in the bulrushes outside the prison walls. "Freedom? Strange, I've had everything but freedom," Ahmad confesses. "And I've had nothing—but freedom," says Abu. Together they will sail along the river to Basra.

Basra is ruled by an aged sultan who has an only daughter, a ravishingly

185

beautiful princess. For a commoner to look upon her face means death. But from hiding Ahmad steals a glimpse of her while she is riding in a procession (archers have carefully cleared the streets before her) and the young king loses his heart. The next day he steals into her garden and, hidden in the branches of a tree above a pond, lets her think his reflection in the water below is actually a djinni. But it is a brief deception. The exiled king and the young princess fall instantly, deeply in love.

"Where have you come from?" she asks. "From the other side of time—to find you," he replies. He has been searching since the beginning of time and will stay with her until time's end. "For me there can be no more beauty in the world, but yours."

He promises to return tomorrow but the princess cautions him: "There is a gardener here who watches night and day. His name is Death." But she cannot forbid him. "Tomorrow!" he calls. *"And all tomorrows,"* she whispers.

However, on the morrow, Jaffar the usurper visits the sultan of Basra,

"Wind!" Jaffar cries, and a cloudless sky becomes overcast, storming on command (left). The sultan, below, embraces another of Jaffar's toys—a ravishing six-armed dervish.

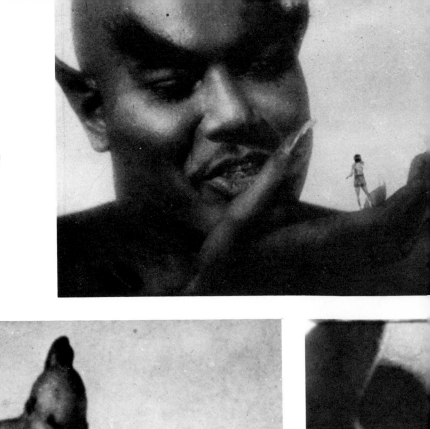
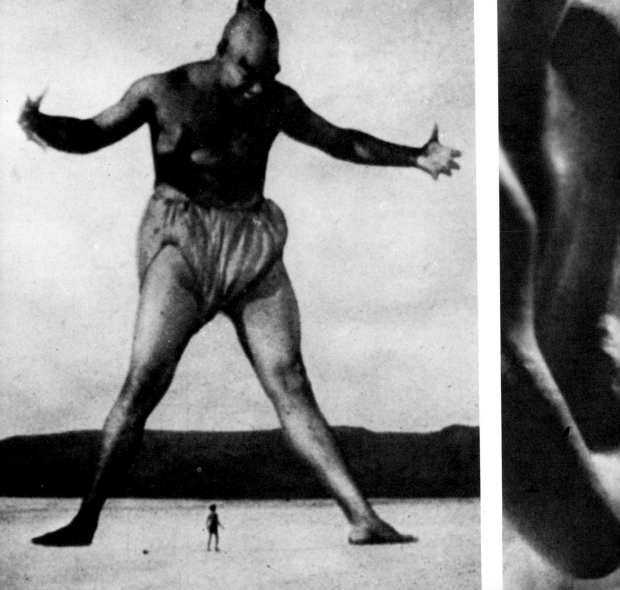

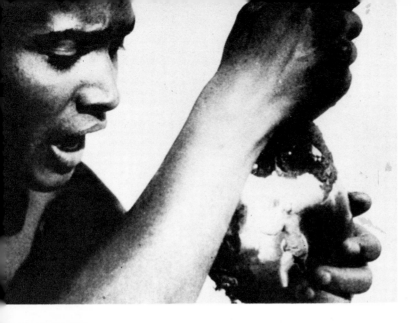

"Free—after two thousand years!" cries the djinni (lower left), but Abu soon tricks him—briefly—back into his bottle (left). Below, Abu hitches an airborne trip.

The djinni brings Abu to the temple of the Goddess of Light, and as a strange tribe watches (right), the young thief steals the All-Seeing Eye.

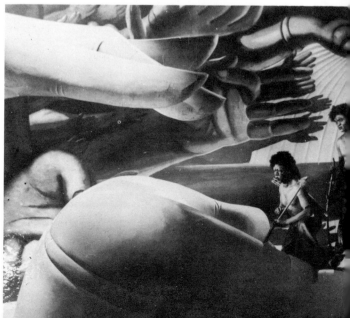

Ahmad fights for the life of his princess, while Abu sails to the rescue astride his flying carpet.

bringing with him some exotic toys as gifts for the old man. The most fantastic toy is a life-size mechanical horse, which, when wound up, actually flies. "I must have this," begs the sultan. Jaffar purrs, "I ask but one thing in return—your daughter." He has seen her beauty in his crystal, for he is a dabbler in magic. The old man shrugs helplessly and consents; he must have the toy horse.

But the princess, having, to her dismay, observed this scene from the women's quarters, vows never to marry this strange and sinister man. Her heart belongs to Ahmad. Disguised as a boy, she makes her escape on horseback. Servants bring word to her father that the princess has vanished.

An immediate search of the palace is ordered, and Ahmad and Abu are found in the garden. Brought before the sultan and the vizier, Ahmad accuses Jaffar of usurping his throne. "My eyes have been witness to his treachery," the young king cries. Jaffar gestures with his hand, and Ahmad is struck blind. Jaffar gestures again, and Abu is changed into a mongrel dog. Not until Jaffar holds the princess in his arms will the spells be broken.

Weeks pass. Months. The fugitive princess is captured by slave traders and brought back to Basra, where she is sold—to Jaffar. But she has slipped into a strange trance, and Jaffar's triumph is hollow. He knows only Ahmad's embrace can rouse her. So he sends an emissary to find the blind young beggar and his mongrel dog.

Ahmad is led to the bed where the princess lies in her endless slumber. She moves, and mutters, "My djinni of the garden, where are you?" And he replies, "I've come from the other side of time to find you." Instantly her eyes open, and they embrace. But *his* eyes—they are so strange, she says uneasily. Ahmad replies, "One cannot go through fire and not be scorched."

The emissary hurries in; the master is returning and Ahmad must go. But he leaves behind his dog: "You not only belong to me now but to the princess as well; guard her." As the beggar is led away, the princess realizes the worst. "Blind!"

The emissary whispers, "It is in your power to restore his sight. There is a doctor . . ." The princess allows herself and the dog to be taken to the harbor,

and on board a massive galleon. The princess is brought to a cabin, and the ship sets sail. Its master is Jaffar.

The mongrel is the first to sense danger. A crewman picks the dog up by the scruff of its neck. The animal growls. Jaffar smiles. "Strange how an unpleasant child can become a decent dog. Throw it overboard!" Then he enters the princess's cabin. "*I* am that doctor. The same moment that you hold me in your arms, Ahmad will see." The princess shivers and closes her eyes: "Hold me in your arms." Like a spider enveloping his prey, Jaffar embraces her.

At that moment, on shore, Ahmad screams in pain. He can see! And a dog that has just swum in from the open sea is transformed into a boy! But all Ahmad can perceive is Jaffar's ship on the horizon. "What good are my eyes to me without her?" In a frenzy, he and Abu set out in an open skiff.

Aboard the galleon, Jaffar is frowning at his passive captive. "I have powers that can force you to my will, but I want more than they can give. I want your *love.*" He pulls her to him. "Forget Ahmad. He has forgotten you." The princess frees herself and runs to the deck, from which she sees the sail of the skiff. Ahmad has not

Captured, Ahmad is shackled in the lowest dungeon, facing his beloved princess. The next day he is led to the scaffold.

forgotten her!

But Jaffar is at the helm of his ship, his arms raised to the heavens as if to pull the sky down upon the sea. He is conjuring up a storm. *"Wind!"* he calls, and a cloudless blue sky becomes overcast and black. Invisible turbulence whips his dark cape around him as he gestures again. *"Waves!"* he calls, and the ocean turns into a shifting, erupting mountain range. The skiff overturns; Ahmad and Abu are tossed into the churning sea.

It is morning, and we find Abu lying on the sands of a deserted beach. Ahmad is nowhere to be found. And Jaffar's great ship has returned to Basra. . . .

The palace garden is now choked with weeds, but the princess spends all her time there, under the watchful and concerned eye of her father. She does not want to go with Jaffar to Bagdad, and she shan't, the old sultan promises: "Never, not while *I* live!" So Jaffar prepares for the sultan one final toy: a beautiful six-armed dervish. "Her embrace will thrill you as no other woman ever has—or will." The sultan eagerly throws himself upon her bosom. Five arms encircle him, while the sixth plunges a jeweled dagger into his back. "Guards," Jaffar commands, "make ready for Bagdad."

On the deserted beach, Abu finds an encrusted bottle. He pulls the stopper and is thrown back by a rush of billowing smoke. The smoke forms into a djinni hundreds of feet high! *"Free*—free after two thousand years!" Twenty centuries ago King Solomon, lord of all the djinn, imprisoned him within the bottle. "For the first thousand years I swore to enrich the one who freed me with all the riches of the earth; but in the second thousand years my imprisoned spirit swore vengeance for all who lived and were free!" He is about to kill Abu, by stepping on him, when the quick-witted

Abu will have none of the fine schooling a grateful Ahmad thrusts on him: "I'm going to find what *I* want—some fun and adventure at last!"

little thief taunts him: "You were never in that bottle! Impossible!"

"Dog of an unbeliever, you shall see that with me nothing is impossible," the djinni cries, and he returns into the small bottle. Laughing, Abu puts the stopper back on: "Just because you were bigger than me, you thought you could bully!" He is just about to cast the bottle into the sea, when the penitent djinni promises to fulfill three wishes for the boy if he will release him. Abu frees the djinni once more, and an uneasy truce begins between them.

Abu's first and rather hasty wish is for some sausages like those his mother used to make. It gratifies his hunger, but he realizes it is rather spendthrift. Abu wants to find out where Ahmad is, but to know that one must look into the All-Seeing Eye, the djinni explains, which not even he can steal. *Steal?* Abu needs no help in that department. "Take me to the Eye—but, mind you, it's not my second wish!" The djinni with Abu holding onto a lock of his hair, jumps into the air and flies away.

Together they soar to the highest peak of the highest mountain of the world, where the earth meets the sky. There is the temple of the Dawn, and in the great hall of the temple is the Goddess of Light, and in the head of the goddess is the All-Seeing Eye. The djinni gently sets his small companion on the ground before an incrediby ornate and massive structure, its silent stones hewn by some forgotten race. From every quarter peer dark dwarves. The djinni pushes Abu through the great jeweled doors. "Now, my little braggart, you can be a thief and a hero all in one!"

The statue of the goddess is huge; so immense are its proportions that one can barely perceive the shining, blood-red All-Seeing Eye high in her forehead. The statue is hollow, and to get to the head Abu must climb a deadly interior spider web. Halfway up he battles the giant spider, cutting it loose from its thread so that it falls into an octopus pit far below. Emerging from one of the goddess's eyes, he climbs up over her forehead and plucks the glowing ruby from its center!

Immediately the temple grows dark, and the strange race of guardians begin an awesome chant. Abu flees to the waiting djinni, who is impressed. "Not for two thousand years will the goddess grow another Eye!" Abu sees Ahmad within the Eye: the young king is lost in a desolate rock canyon. "Take me to him," Abu commands—his second wish. "Hold tight, little brother; we must return halfway around the world!"

Admad, clambering across the lifeless rocks of a narrow crevice, is amazed when his young friend is lowered down to him by the huge djinni. "He is mine—I am his master," Abu boasts, and the djinni laughs menacingly. Abu fully realizes he has only one wish left, and that he must be careful. Ahmad moans that his only wish is to see his princess again, to which Abu delightedly replies, "That's easy, just look hard into this All-Seeing Eye. . . ."

In the ruby stone, Ahmad sees Jaffar's palace at Bagdad . . . sees the princess . . . and sees her approach a strange blue rose. "I've heard of that!

The blue rose of forgetfulness. One whiff of its fragrance, and she'll forget *everything!*" Ahmad, in the Eye, sees her bring the flower to her face, and watches still as Jaffar approaches. "Who are you?" he asks the girl. "I do not know," she replies. "Why have you suffered?" he asks. "Have I suffered?"

Ahmad is rent with grief. "Why have you shown me this?" he shouts at Abu. The boy protests he only stole it to be of help, but Ahmad is in a vicious mood. "You stole it because you enjoy stealing! I wish I were dead! I—I wish I were in Bagdad!" Abu turns upon him: "I wish you were too!"

And Ahmad vanishes.

It was Abu's third wish. With a roar of laughter that makes the rocks shake, the djinni soars heavenward. "Free! *Free!*" Abu is left alone in a deserted world.

At Jaffar's palace in Bagdad, Ahmad suddenly materializes. The house guards—an army of them—swarm over him, and he is captured. His only reward is one more quick glimpse of his beloved, and the knowledge the blue rose has failed in its work: she recognizes him. The infuriated Jaffar has reached the limits of his patience, and his attempts to win the love of the princess have come to an end. "Tomorrow at dawn they will die together."

At dawn, both Ahmad and the princess are spread-eagled against the dungeon walls, waiting the end. But at least they are together, and Ahmad would rather be with his beloved in death than without her in life. If only he and Abu had not parted quarreling! Abu, still in the rock crevices and aware of Ahmad's fate through the All-Seeing Eye, is full of despair. In tears, he smashes the Eye down against the canyon wall. To his surprise, the world turns upside down!

He suddenly finds himself in a golden city of tents in a sunlit valley, a city presided over by a gathering of old men with white beards, one of whom greets him: "Welcome, little prince. For you we have been waiting twice two thousand years." Abu protests: he is not a prince, but just a thief. However, "This is the land of legend, where everything is possible, when seen through the eyes of youth. We are the remnants of the Golden Age...." Abu is awestruck, but the ancient wise man continues: "We were petrified with horror when men ceased to become children and believe in the beauty of the impossible. Whenever the heart of a child comes to us, we live again. As that child, you are to be my successor."

The kindly old man presents the bewildered boy, as his successor, with two insignia of true kingship. The first is a silver crossbow, "Aim this only at injustice, and you cannot fail." The second is a carpet, "which flies when it is ridden." But it must not be taken away, for it still belongs to the ancient king, who will be borne to Paradise on it at his appointed hour.

At Bagdad, the sun rises over the city spires. The populace gathers for an execution.

Alone with the carpet, Abu raises his eyes to heaven and Allah. "I know You don't much like stealing, but when the old king's hour comes, You, O Allah, will take him by the hand. I must use this carpet to save my friend...." The ancient king, watching unseen, smiles. *"Fly!"* commands Abu.

At Jaffar's palace, Ahmad is led to the scaffold. Suddenly Abu on his carpet soars across the great squares (where the prophets are still saying, "This shall be the sign of the liberator—he shall be the lowest of the low, and you shall look for him in the clouds"). The city is thrown into pandemonium and rebellion at the sight of the boy riding the flying carpet. Jaffar, sensing the end, makes for his magic horse, mounts it, and gallops away high above the rooftops of Bagdad. Abu aims his crossbow, and an arrow pierces Jaffar's forehead.

Days later, before a cheering populace, King Ahmad shouts, "My people, I owe everything to Abu, and when he is grown he shall be my grand vizier. He shall be sent to the best schools in Bagdad, and all the wise men of the East shall teach him the wisdom of the world." But Abu will have none of this. He is uncomfortable in his royal robes. Clambering onto his carpet, he sails into a rainbow. "You've found what you wanted, now I'm going to find what *I* want—some fun and adventure at last!" And the little thief of Bagdad is gone.

No picture less reflects twentieth-century styles of warfare than *The Thief of Bagdad*, yet it was released to a public on the brink of World War II. It certainly could not compete with that conflict's real-life horrors, and yet, fragile and fantastic as it is, it found an audience that accepted its wonders as a welcome escape from the realities of marching invaders against which would sail no liberator astride a magic carpet. *The Thief of Bagdad* is one of the few great epic romances of our time—the screen's own *Thousand-and-One-Nights* tale—a great contribution to the cinema of the fantastic.

BEAUTY AND THE BEAST

(La Belle et la Bête)

The Beast/Avenant	Jean Marais
Beauty	Josette Day
The Merchant	Marcel André
Felicity	Nane Germon
Adelaide	Mila Parely
Ludovic	Michel Auclair

Direction, story, and dialogue by Jean Cocteau
Director of Production: Emile Darbon
Based on the tale by Madame Leprince de Beaumont
Music: Georges Auric
Editor: Claude Ibéria
A Discina release of an André Paulve Production

Released (in the United States) January 15, 1948; French release January, 1946

Ugliness breeds ugliness. On the "home front" during World War II, the American film industry descended into an orgy of horror cinema. For the first time in a decade work was plentiful, yet demanding. War-created tensions were high, and movies provided practically the only release and escape. There were musicals and romances, to be sure, but every studio had its growing retinue of mad doctors, deformed monsters, insane killers, victims ill-met by moonlight. The "escape" drama of these violent times seemed to demand blood sacrifice. It was from France that an antidote came. There, at war's end, a poet named Jean Cocteau fashioned out of the simplest materials a fantasy film that stands as a classic for the ages, drawing for his source on an elemental fairy tale and proving to a scarred and weary world, a world nearly leveled by battle, that a beautiful flower *does* sometimes grow in rubble.

Cocteau had directed only one film

199

before, and this many years previously, in 1930: an expressionistic journey of a sleepwalker through a nightmare world, *Blood of a Poet (Le Sang d'un Poète,* released in 1932). Born in 1891, Cocteau had been one of the great creators and innovators of French letters, starting fresh currents and whole new movements in literature, painting, music, theater, and the ballet. He was to leave a mark on films as well. The weird, dreamlike *Blood of a Poet,* much of it set in a hotel corridor down which the poet glides both to observe and to work out strange fancies, even killing himself to serve artistic tradition, was a stunning success, and it ranked among the most famous of avant-garde classics. But by now Cocteau was well into an anxious middle age, having survived a damaging, spirit-defeating war, and especially a claustrophobic occupation. It was not a unique survival—all France had done so—but Cocteau was especially sensitive to the war's disorder. He had begun to feel he was slipping from the public view, despite the mild success of a film he had written during the war years, a complex allegory called *The Eternal Return (L'Eternel Retour,* 1943). It had renewed his interest in film and given him a feeling that a cinema project would revitalize him, strengthen him.

But rather than a film with obtuse meanings and clouded themes, he would construct a motion picture on the simplest level, a fairy story taken from French legend, full of pageantry and poetry. He could not have chosen more wisely. To a wounded age shaking itself free from a disastrous war, *Beauty and the Beast,* with its innocence and hope, was an ideal healing potion; for succeeding ages it has become a classic in the cinema of the fantastic.

And yet Cocteau often insisted that his films were not fantastic, which in his journals he defined as that which

"separates us from the limitations within which we have to live." Too often, he complained, people would confuse mere stage trickery with true magic and would ask him to write about film fantasy because of creations like *Beauty and the Beast* in which many see "the projection of that curiosity which impels me to open forbidden doors, to walk in the dark and sing to keep up my courage. . . ." But the true fantasy of that film, Cocteau maintained, was not in fairies and abracadabra, but in the way that—as in all fairy stories—things are accepted as normal that would never be normal in our mundane world. The *enchantment* of *Beauty and the Beast* mesmerizes us, removes us from the here and now, and transports us to a very real world of its own. . . .

It took a half year to film *Beauty and the Beast.* Much of it was shot at Rochecorbon, a small manor in the Loire valley that closely matched Cocteau's images of Beauty's home. The great French film director René Clément was Cocteau's "adviser" on the project, and the Beast was portrayed by Cocteau's closest friend, Jean Marais, the dynamic, heroic young actor whose career the poet had long guided. (Beauty was aptly cast as well; actress Josette Day's features were both sensitive and patrician.) Jean Marais insisted that his Beast makeup not be a mask but instead be applied, fur hair and all, directly to his face. Frequently this would take five hours and would be agony both for Cocteau and the actor, for it was Cocteau who most often administered the lion's-head makeup—who did everything, in fact, from building props to moving equipment.

For the poet it was an painful and terrible time. The production was beset with difficulty: bad weather, inadequate lighting and facilities, sickness that spread through the cast.

Cocteau kept a journal of the film's making, and it is a record of suffering. And yet the poet, being a poet, knew that suffering is not always wasted, that it can be kneaded like yeast into the creative forces. And that the result is sometimes the better for it.

Children believe what we tell them. They have implicit faith. They believe the plucking of a rose may bring disaster to a family. They believe the hands of a human beast begin to smoke after a killing, and that the beast is put to shame by this when a young girl dwells in his house. They believe in a host of other simple things.

It is some of this simple faith that I ask of you, and to bring good luck to us all, let me say to you four magic words, the true "Open Sesame" of childhood: Once upon a Time . . .

So Cocteau begins his fairy tale, and immediately we are plunged into the chattering, everyday world of a provincial manor on a sunlit, ordinary day in the seventeenth century. The two proud older daughters of the house are trying on gowns, abusing stable boys, and scolding their brother and his friend, hunting outside, whose arrows have come too close. Actually, it is a troubled household: the father, a merchant, has lost his ships and faces ruin. The youngest daughter, called Beauty, does the work of the house, serving her sisters and doing their share because they are lovely and have fine hands. Avenant, the friend of Beauty's brother, pleads with Beauty to marry him, but she will not leave her father.

The father, who has gone to the port to meet his last ship, finds his creditors have seized everything. He must return home alone through a dark and mysterious forest. Night falls rapidly; ground fog swirls about him and his horse, obscuring all paths, while thunder sounds sinisterly through the trees. He is lost and frightened. Suddenly he comes upon a manor house. There is no one in the well-lit courtyard. He enters the house and is engulfed in a mist, from which he emerges to find a great banqueting hall, with a meal laid on and a fire blazing merrily. It is illuminated by candelabra held in human hands jutting from the stone walls. Shaking with fear, he sees one arm obligingly wave him toward the table. He seats himself, still fearful, and more hands, apparently growing from the table, reach out to pour his wine and serve his dinner, while the faces carved on the fireplace look on with human eyes.

Times passes. The father has fallen into a groggy sleep, and he wakens with a start. All is still. He hurries back through the great hall—dark now, and smoky, as the candles have been extinguished—and finds himself in the manor garden, with dawn outlining a bush of white roses. He remembers that the only present his daughter Beauty has asked him to bring home from his journey was a rose—so he breaks one from the bush. At that moment, an incredible figure, his body a man's, powerful, broad-shouldered, yet his head that of an animal, leaps into his way. *"So! You are stealing my roses,"* the creature snarls, *"the treasures I prize most in the world. You could have taken anything but my roses. It so happens this simple theft is punishable by death."*

The father falls to his knees, pleading for his life; the garden has suddenly grown chill, and an autumn wind sweeps brittle leaves across a clouded landscape. "My Lord," the terrified man pleads, and the fanged monster interrupts him: "Do not call me 'My Lord,' Call me *'Beast.'* I detest compliments." The father is to die in fifteen minutes . . . unless . . . unless

201

Jean Cocteau, looking extremely earnest, joins members of his company on the set.

one of his daughters . . . How many has he? Three, the old man whimpers. Unless, the Beast growls, one of his daughters will agree to pay the penalty in his place. Grasping at straws, the father vows either he or one of his daughters will be back in three days. But how will he find his way out of this terrible forest, in which he is already lost? The Beast tells him to take a white horse from the stables, an animal called Magnificent, and to whisper in its ear, *"Go where I am going, Magnificent. Go, go, go."* The old man stumbles toward the stable, leaving the Beast alone in his garden amid the swirling leaves.

When the father returns home, he tells his daughters of the strange happening. Beauty's sharp-tongued older sisters immediately berate her for causing the misadventure: "Imagine the *arrogance!* Asking for *roses!*" Of course Beauty, a good and loving daughter, insists on offering herself in her father's stead; she would rather die herself than suffer the sorrow of his loss. But he will hear none of this.

The next day the girl, cloaked and hooded, moves silently into the stable and climbs on Magnificent, whispering the magic command. At once the wise white steed gallops with her out of the village and into the dark wood. By night they are at the manor gates, and Beauty moves into the strange hall; the

202

hands holding candelabra motion her upstairs. Here she finds herself in a long corridor, illuminated by moonlight falling through windows with billowing translucent curtains. She hears a soft voice: "Beauty, I am the door to your room." It is a handsome room, but invaded by trees and wild flowers. "I am your mirror, Beauty," the small, ornate looking glass on her dressing table whispers to her, and in the glass the girl sees her father in his bed, tossing in a troubled sleep. She flees from the room and down a massive stone staircase to a dark courtyard. She is almost at the gates when they are flung open, and the towering Beast, his cape like bat's wings, moves quickly into her path. *Where are you going?"* he rages. It is the most frightening thing she has ever seen, and Beauty faints

The great man-animal circles the prone girl and swoops her up into his arms. With surprising tenderness he carries her through the candlelit great hall and to her room, laying her across the regal bed. His hairy, fanged face studies the unconscious girl. Suddenly her eyes flutter and open, and he jumps away, startled. "Beauty, you must not look into my eyes," he rasps. "Have no fear. You shall see me but once every evening—at seven o'clock. I shall visit you as you dine." And then the Beast disappears, back into the shadows.

It is seven. Beauty is alone in the Great Hall before the roaring fireplace, at the resplendent table from which the bodiless hands serve her a meal she hardly touches. She is suddenly aware the Beast has come up behind her. "Do not be afraid," he whispers throatily. "Will you let me watch you dine?" Steeling herself, Beauty replies with

Beauty's sisters demonstrate their elegance and hauteur.

closed eyes, "You are the master." To this she hears the surprising response, "No. There is but one master here. You." It is a strange dinner, during which the Beast makes his confession. "I am a monster, and I'm lacking in wit," the Beast groans, but the girl says he has the wit to recognize this. The Beast retreats, reminding her that he will visit her just once each evening, and always with the same question: will she be his wife? Beauty declines with a shiver. The Beast moves backward through a dark passage that looks strangely like the entrance to a cage.

In her lonely, frightened explorations of castle and grounds—which often seem caught in some cloudy twilight—Beauty sometimes catches a glimpse of her tormented host, his face contorted with some secret agony, his talons smoking, or lying on the ground, like an animal, lapping water from a pool. Once she finds him in her room; he stammers that he wanted to bring her a gift and thrusts a priceless necklace at her before hurrying away. In the days that pass, she asks to join him in his walks; when they are by the pool and the Beast is thirsty, she lets him drink from her cupped hands. Gradually her fear of the Beast subsides, and she knows she will do nothing to make him suffer. She begins to look forward anxiously to seven o'clock, and when the Beast is late, the faces flanking the fireplace peer at the girl as she paces back and forth.

Beauty's father rides alone through the dark, mysterious forest and comes upon a strange castle. The frightened merchant walks through a hall lit by candles held by human hands.

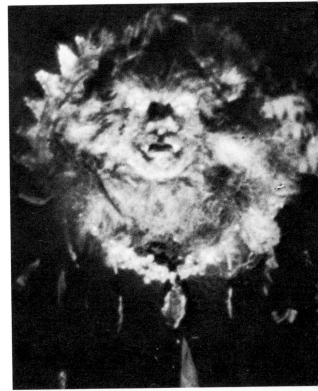

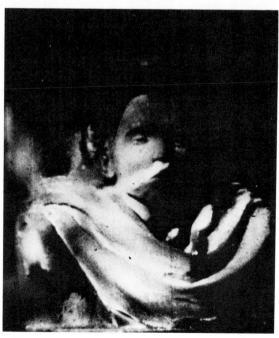

But Beauty, no longer afraid, is still unhappy. She has seen her father in the magic mirror and knows he is dying. She pleads with the Beast to allow her to return home for one last visit. At first he refuses, but then he makes her vow to return in one week. "If you do not, *I will die.*" He takes her to a balcony and points out a small pavilion in the mists. All he owns, he owns by magic, but his actual wealth is locked in the pavilion. Should he die, it will all become hers. To show his confidence in her return, he gives her the key. "A rose, my mirror, my golden key, my horse, and this glove—these are the five secrets of my power. You have only to put the glove on your right hand, and you'll be taken wherever you will. Remember your promise." And the Beast bids her farewell.

Beauty pulls on the rough black glove—and is immediately transported into her father's bedroom, in the familiar house already stripped bare by creditors. She tells her surprised father of her life with the Beast. "Father, this monster is good." She is happy—or would be if she could make him forget his ugliness. As she speaks of her feelings for her captor, the tears she sheds for his suffering and loneliness

The merchant sits down to a magical meal, served by hands without a body; he is spied upon by sculpted faces with human eyes.

turn into tiny diamonds. She asks her
father not to tell her sisters of the
jewels, for they will take them from
him. Indeed, Beauty's two sisters,
smarting in their new poverty, do not
take kindly to their returned Beauty,
now blossomed from plainness to a
court lady! When one sister admires
Beauty's necklace, Beauty offers it to
her—"it would look even finer on
you"—but the rich strands of pearl turn
into a smoking rope. The necklace was
meant only for Beauty. She reveals she
has promised to return at the end of
the week, or else the Beast will surely
die. Besides, she has the key to his
treasure.

Storm clouds brew over Beauty's
visit home. Her handsome young village
suitor, Avenant (played, as is the Beast,
by Jean Marais), jealous of the liking
and sympathy she expresses for the

Home again, the
shaken merchant
gives Beauty—
notice her
plain clothes—the
rose he has taken
from the manor
garden (upper left).
To pay the price
for the rose,
Beauty goes to the
sinister manor in
her father's stead,
riding on a magical
horse through the
dark forest
(above).

Beast, finds the idea of her return intolerable. He vows to find his way to the monster's home and kill him. Avenant and Ludovic enlist the help of Beauty's sisters, who, pretending to weep, protest their love for her and persuade her to stay another week. But at the same time they secretly steal the golden key to the Beast's treasure! As soon as they have it, they turn against her. Beauty is troubled and sad, and Avenant blames the Beast, telling her that if the Beast were really suffering at her absence, he would come to find her; but he has forgotten her.

We see the Beast prowling through Beauty's deserted room, alone in his silent mansion, clutching the coverlet of her bed to his breast. But the girl does not return.

Beauty's treacherous sisters and brother and the vengeful Avenant conspire to find a way to the Beast's domain, for they are all unsure of the paths through the enchanted forest. They hear a clatter in the stable yard: it is the horse Magnificent, sent to fetch Beauty. Beauty had told them of the animal and its password; Avenant and Ludovic climb upon the animal and speed off—Avenant to challenge the Beast to battle for Beauty's freedom, while Ludovic plots to loot the treasure. Unaware of this, Beauty lies weeping on her bed, and then in her enchanted mirror she sees her Beast. He is dying. The mirror shatters. Horror-stricken, Beauty pulls on the magic glove and in an instant is back in the somber passageways of the Beast's world.

"Beast! My Beast!" she calls, but he is nowhere. She finds him at last in the garden, lying by an autumnal pond, the object of furious investigation by a cluster of swans. "Do not die; you must *live!*" Beauty pleads, but it is too late. The Beast turns to her weakly. If he were a man, he would have the strength and courage to fight on, but poor

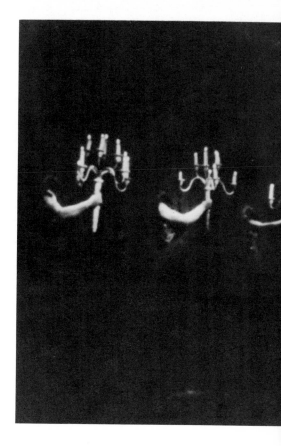

A wind sets the curtains in the
passage billowing; the apprehensive
Beauty flees through the halls.
Suddenly the Beast appears. It is
the most frightening thing Beauty
has ever seen. She faints
(overleaf).

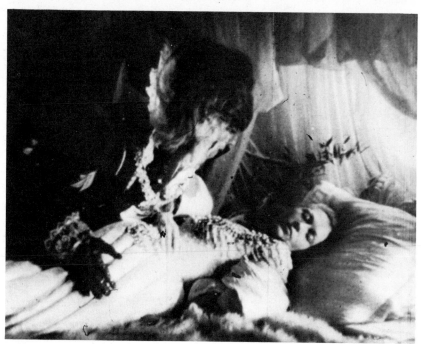

Tenderly the Beast carries the
unconscious girl to her regal bed (above).
Every evening they meet.
"Will you be my wife?"

Beauty comforts the Beast (upper left). A guardian statue of Diana comes to life and fires her arrow (above center) at the intruder Avenant; it pierces his heart (right). His face becomes beastlike—and as it does so, the Beast also changes. . . .

beasts can only show their love by lying down on the ground and dying. His head falls to one side, as Beauty, sobbing, swears that she loves him and will be his wife.

At that very moment, Avenant and Ludovic are breaking into the treasure pavilion. Fearful of a trap, they have decided not to use the key but to climb in by way of the roof. Through a glass skylight they gaze at the brilliant treasure, watched over by a statue of Diana, the virgin huntress. Avenant breaks the glass pane and swings down, but as he hangs in midair an arrow from Diana's bow pierces his back and he falls down onto the treasure. Dying, his face contorts and is hideously changed into that of a beast—the Beast.

But the Beast is himself miraculously transformed. As a high wind rises, seeming to sweep away the terror and the darkness, the body lying by the garden pool, suddenly radiant, rises to its feet. No longer a Beast, a handsome young man the very image of Avenant,

clad in princely raiment, stands before Beauty.

Beauty shrinks back in terror. The young man reaches out to her. "The Beast is no more. It was I. A loving look alone could turn me into a man. Love can make a man a beast—love can also beautify ugliness." He takes Beauty in his arms. Does she miss his ugliness? The first time he held her in his arms it was as the Beast. But she is unafraid. He will take her to his kingdom, where she'll be a queen, and her sisters will serve her. "Come with me," he says, and together, locked in an embrace, they are lifted magically into the clouds and float, two enchanted lovers, from our gaze forever.

Beauty and the Beast won for Jean Cocteau the Prix Louis Delluc and several prizes at the Cannes Film Festival. It played an important part in electing Cocteau to the French Academy nine years later, in 1955. The

219

The enchanted lovers float up into the clouds. "Love can beautify ugliness."

poet died in 1963, and while he was to complete several more film projects none would be a close return to the simple strengths of a fairy tale.

The niche occupied by *Beauty and the Beast* among fantasy classics is special. Few films have been less imitated, for its time came and went almost instantly. When it first appeared it filled a need by chasing horror from a

Europe wracked by a war that had finally ended. But the postwar sigh of relief was of short duration. New uncertainties, tensions, and outright terrors were to darken the sun, and the cinema of the fantastic would take new directions. The simple and the true and the good—these qualities were no longer enough.

THE THING

(The Thing from Another World)

Captain Patrick Hendry	Kenneth Tobey
Nikki Nicholson	Margaret Sheridan
Carrington	Robert Cornthwaite
Scotty (Ned Scott)	Douglas Spencer
Lieutenant Eddie Dykes	James Young
Crew Chief (Bob)	Dewey Martin
Lieutenant MacPherson	Robert Nichols
Sergeant Barnes	William Self
Dr. Stern	Eduard Franz
Mrs. Chapman	Sally Creighton
and	
The Thing	James Arness

Directed by Christian Nyby
Produced by Howard Hawks
Screenplay by Charles Lederer
Based on the story "Who Goes There?" by John W. Campbell, Jr.
Director of Photography: Russell Harlan, ASC
Music: Dimitri Tiomkin
A Winchester Pictures Corporation Presentation

Released by RKO March, 1951

The late forties were a period of American paranoia, and many had difficulty adjusting to the first years of what was called the postatomic age. The growing hysteria of "the flying saucer menace" was symptomatic of a countrywide unrest over the achievements of science and the point to which it had brought us. The destruction of the world and

A strange aircraft of some kind has crashed into the Artic ice; its tail fin still protrudes (left). Its shape—the men join hands to determine its outline—is a perfect circle (below). Suddenly, the craft self-destructs.

extraterrestrial invasion—two of the dominant motifs of the period—clearly demonstrated our anxiety over the increasing complexities of the time. It remained for a single film to exploit both neurotic themes. Happily, the film was a great one.

Its producer also had greatness about him. Since the thirties no one in Hollywood more symbolized in his work rugged, undaunted masculinity than the aggressive Howard Hawks. In nearly every film genre that featured men in conflict Hawks created classics—crime melodramas like *Scarface* (1932) or the adaptation of Raymond Chandler's *The Big Sleep* (1946), war dramas like *The Road to Glory* (1936) and *Sergeant York* (1941), air dramas like *Only Angels Have Wings* (1939), rough battle-of-the-sexes comedies like *His Girl Friday* (1940), and, especially, great Westerns such as *Red River* (1948). Hawks believed that the essence of drama was the pitting of strong, individualistic men against demanding odds within a stark setting. He enjoyed working in the simplistic Western form where tough men faced (with few weapons except their own courage, loyalty, and camaraderie) a nearly overwhelmingly hostile nature. And it was Howard Hawks's theory that this energetic style of storytelling, these characteristics and conflicts so suitable to the Western, could be transposed to a totally different story form: the science fiction genre.

Hawks was one of the first to see the screen possibilities of the postwar publishing upswing in science fiction. He had purchased one of the more heralded stories in this new writing category, *Who Goes There?* which John W. Campbell, Jr., the editor of the foremost magazine in the field, *Astounding Science Fiction,* had first written back in 1938. (The magazine is now called *Analog* and was still edited by Campbell, until his death in 1971; he was an astonishingly vigorous

explorer of new ideas and wild scientific horizons.)

Basically—as with nearly all Campbell's crisp, thoughtful writing—*Who Goes There?* posed a problem to be solved. A group of men on an Antarctic expedition come upon a creature—an alien life form from some crashed extraterrestial ship—frozen into the ice, they surmise, for millions of years. They dig it out; it returns to life and quickly begins to consume both sled dogs and human beings, in each case perfectly duplicating both the shapes and the thoughts of the beings it has absorbed! It can go on endlessly until it takes the world. How can one recognize it in order to stop it?

The problem that Campbell posed, Hawks was not to solve. Hawks, instead, took the polar expedition with its opportunities for close-order comradeship, hearty masculinity, and a struggle against a dangerous natural terrain (he changed the setting from the Antarctic to the North Pole), and pitted the expedition against a somewhat different enemy. *The Thing from Another World* states its case in its title: the enemy is not human; it is an alien *thing*.

Ready to meet this frightening foe is nothing so abstract as science; the challenger is the United States military. Often, in the routine science fiction films of this period and later, the world is saved by, say, the Marines, but in no other film is the heroism, the professionalism, and the effectiveness of "our side" so earnestly and dramatically portrayed. The courage and pragmatism of brave but ordinary men on a combat mission against the unknown, of an order somewhat

reminiscent of cavalry soldiers facing overwhelming odds in a grand-scale Western, and featuring the aggressive and supermasculine heroes who were a Hawks specialty, made the film one of the big box-office successes of its day—and a gripping classic in the cinema of terror, a starkly real set piece of man's struggle against the nonhuman portrayed with mounting, knuckle-whitening suspense.

And yet, as landmark science fiction fantasy, *The Thing** is curiously anti-science. Over and over again the scientists are portrayed as men of weak and ineffectual ideas, while the soldiers are men of action. The scientists wish to communicate with and understand the alien; the military wants only to defend and destroy. Harks sides with the latter view. (He later claimed the anti-science feelings of the screenplay were not planned but just seemed to make a better story.)

The film also contains curious propaganda for the actual possibility of extraterrestrial invasion. At a time when many parts of the nation were already near hysteria over flying saucer sightings (great fleets of UFOs were being spotted with regularity), the ending of *The Thing,* in which a reporter squarely facing the audience warns of extraterrestrial comings, seriously exploited this national anxiety.

Officially Howard Hawks was only the producer of *The Thing,* but for years it has been rumored that he also directed large portions of it. (The competent Christian Nyby, listed as director, had previously been Hawks's film editor; he went on to do some minor Westerns and much television work.) The male ethos, the driving

---

*The film starts in darkness; slowly the fiery letters of the words *THE THING* eat their way across the screen. Then the smaller words *from Another World* appear across the bottom—looking like a cautious afterthought on the part of RKO executives, to make sure there would be no mistaking the title's meaning: an alien visitation. The film has been referred to by RKO under both titles.

Reporter Scotty
(second from left in
illustration left)
looks on as Dr.
Carrington (in fur
cap) and Pat Hendry
(right) investigate
their bizarre find—a
being from another
world frozen into the
ice! There is time for
a romantic
interlude between
Hendry and Nikki
(lower left). Later,
the camp makes an
unsettline discovery:
the creature is alive
—and has escaped
from the thawed
ice block.

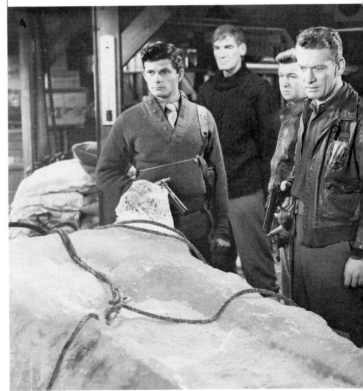

The alien strikes inside the camp. In the snow, one of the creature's arms—which a dog has bitten off—is found (above).

dialogue with overlapping lines both remind one of Hawks. His cast was made up of unknowns, or at least names without marquee pull: Kenneth Tobey was the hero, and Margaret Sheridan the heroine, a typically Hawksian girl, pleasantly hard, the equal of any man in the struggle between the sexes. Their own private love-war is a minor motif of the film and provides it with its few light moments. As the giant alien Hawks chose a hulking, twenty-nine-year-old bit player, for his size and for his ability to convey menace. The actor was James Arness.

The Thing from Another World begins calmly enough at an Army Air Force base in Anchorage, with the temperature at twenty-five below. We are introduced to young Captain Hendry, a cool professional pilot, and to a middle-aged newspaperman, Scotty, on the outlook for a story but having little luck. Some miles away, in the Arctic cold, an expedition of scientists has built an outpost. Its leader, Dr. Carrington, suddenly radios the base that a strange plane has crashed into the ice. Hendry is assigned to fly to the outpost and manages to

get Scotty aboad the army plane. En route they notice that electrical disturbances have temporarily knocked out all their instruments.

At the scientists's base Pat Hendry runs into another problem—a romantic one. He has had one previous date with "Nikki" Nicholson, secretary to the expedition, and in a brief meeting they amiably discuss how on that occasion, at the Anchorage officers club, she managed to drink him under the table. Still smarting from this loss of masculine superiority, Hendry leaves the girl and introduces himself to Dr. Carrington. The scientist, cold, aloof, exacting, explains that their radar readings registered the crash landing of an immense object into the polar ice. The object moved with the speed of a meteor, and yet it was no meteor, for it hurtled in an upward direction before reversing to crash. The object is estimated to weigh twenty thousand tons: an awful lot of steel for any plane, Hendry protests. "Any airplane we *know*," corrects Carrington.

They fly over the area where the object has crashed and see in the ice a vast circular shape sealed below the surface. A fantastic craft, with tail fin extending above the surface, has landed, its friction melting the ice, which has then rapidly frozen over it. The fin is of no recognizable metal; the geiger counters are going crazy. The men join hands to determine the outline of the craft. The shape is a nearly perfect circle. "We've finally got one," Scotty exults. "A *flying saucer!*"

Hendry easily assumes command: they will try to melt the ice with thermal bombs. In the meantime Scotty cannot file a story until Air Force Command gives its permission. The thermal bombs are set. "A few minutes from now we may have the key to the stars," Carrington muses; "a million years of history are awaiting us beneath that ice." But as they set off

the charges, the shape under the snow suddenly self-destructs in a blast of flame and smoke.

All are disheartened by this unexpected turn. Scotty mutters darkly about Hendry's wisdom in using "Standard Operating Procedure"—the fire bombs—to thaw out the ship. Carrington bemoans "secrets that might have given us a new science." But the geiger counters pick up something else under the ice. A man—a huge man—who has evidently been thrown clear of the ship but frozen fast: an incredible discovery! "A man from Mars," crows one of the Air Force pilots.

They carefully chop out an

eight-foot-long block of ice, in which the alien is encased, and fly it back to the scientists' polar base. Once there, Carrington immediately wants to thaw out and examine the creature, but Hendry stops him. He has already made one goof and lost the spaceship. Until he receives further instructions from his superior officers, they are going to mark time. Carrington is furious, but another scientist points out that the creature may have brought harmful outer-space microorganisms, disease germs from another planet, and should remain frozen. They leave the alien in his coffin-shaped cake of ice in the base laboratory, where Hendry carefully smashes a window to keep the temperature so low that the creature has no chance to melt free.

An unsettling atmosphere hangs over the base that evening. Hendry has placed a guard over his prize, but the ice has begun to clear, and his men can discern the features of the alien. Hairless, with eyes wide open and seeming to stare, the creature gives the soldiers the jitters. Hendry himself has a rather bad romantic session with Nikki, who, in a typical but incredible Hawksian example of the battle of the sexes, insists the only way they can have a drink together is with Hendry's hands tied behind him, because the last time, he got drunk and pawed her!

Meanwhile, the soldier guarding the ice block has settled down comfortably to read but has unwittingly placed his electric blanket atop the block of ice. The sled dogs howl in the polar blizzard outside. We hear—but the young soldier does not—the steady drip, drip of the melting ice. Suddenly a shadow looms over the soldier, and he looks up. With a scream he pulls his gun and fires, and then he bolts from the room. *"It's alive! That thing isn't dead, it's alive! Those hands . . . those eyes . . .!"* The soldier is hysterical.

When they reenter the room, the alien has gone, fled into the snow. In the screaming blizzard winds they see a dim shape struggling with the sled dogs. Two huskies are found dead, and in their teeth, what looks like an arm! No human arm . . . bloodless, without animal tissue or nerve endings, it is just unconnected cellular growth—like a vegetable. "Just like a super carrot," says Hendry in awe, as the scientists examine their find. Not beyond the range of possibility, Carrington explains; the creature must be from a planet where vegetable life underwent an evolution similar to that of animal life here. "That explains the superiority of its brain. Its development was not handicapped by emotional or sexual factors." Under the nails of the hand are seed pods, and Carrington marvels at the uncomplicated method of reproduction: "No pain . . . no emotions . . . no heart. How superior!"

And suddenly the hand moves. It's alive! It has ingested the canine blood with which it had been covered. "It lives on blood," Scotty moans. Hendry orders an immediate search of the camp. Carrington hangs back, gathers his fellow scientists, and suggests a conspiracy against the military, so that they can be the first to communicate with this superior being who has constructed a ship that has flown millions of miles.

Events happen swiftly. The creature kills more of the dogs, then breaks into the base greenhouse and murders two scientists, *draining them of all their blood.* Carrington, working feverishly and at the point of exhaustion, had planted the hand's seed pods in a tabletop earth culture, feeding the seeds with plasma. In five hours many strange pulsing plants have pushed up through the soil. The other scientists are incredulous at the speed of reproduction. What if the aircraft came here not to visit, but to conquer, "to start growing some horrible army."

228

Carrington wishes to communicate with the alien: "No pain . . . no emotions . . . no heart. How superior!" (upper right). Hendry discovers the scientist's plant growths (upper left) and orders them destroyed. They await the creature's return (below).

Carrington demurs: "There are no enemies in science, only phenomena to be studied."

Hendry learns of the plant growths and orders them destroyed. But how does one destroy the parent—how does one do away with a walking vegetable? "Boil it, bake it, fry it," Nikki suggests. They decide upon burning it with kerosine when its need for blood-food drives it to another attack.

Suddenly the alien bursts through an outer door. Hendry and his men douse the creature with the inflammable fluid and set it ablaze. But with a terrible cry, with flailing, burning arms (they can clearly see it has already grown something of a replacement hand) the alien dashes through a window and manages to smother its flaming body in the snow outside.

It will certainly attack again. This time, however, the men will use something hotter than fire: electricity. Suddenly Nikki notices that the temperature in the base is lowering; the alien has somehow shut off the oil supply that heats the camp's furnaces. Outside, it is sixty below, and in only a matter of an hour or so it will be that cold indoors as well. Hendry speculates that the alien's next logical move will be to tamper with the source of electricity—the generator room. He orders all the camp personnel to barricade the generator, which is at the end of a long corridor along which runs wooden planking. What if the creature could be lured down that corridor, over planks wired to electrocute him . . .

Carrington is horrified at this plan of defense. "You are robbing science of the greatest secrets ever to come to it. Knowledge is more important than life! We owe it to the brain of our species to die rather than to destroy a source of wisdom." "Get him out of here," snaps Hendry.

The geiger counters reveal that the monster is coming closer. Tension mounts, almost making the men forget the increasing cold. The door flings open at the end of the corridor, and there the creature stands—when suddenly the lights go out! Carrington has shut off the generator in an effort to spare the alien from the wired planks. But the others brush him aside and start the power once more. As they do so, however, the scientist uses the diversion to dash toward the alien. "Listen, I'm your friend," Carrington beseeches. "You're wiser than I, you must understand what I'm trying to tell you. They think you mean to harm them; I want to know you, to help you. . . . You're wiser than anything on earth. . . . I'm not your enemy, I'm a scientist—" With one blow the creature sends him reeling to the ground, stunned.

Then the alien moves forward on the walk, to where the electrical trap has been laid. Hendry signals, and three lightninglike currents arc over the bald head and stab into the giant body. The creature screams, and the human beings increase the power coursing through it. Wave after wave of electrical force attacks the being, which slowly crumples to the floor and burns to charred cinder.

The men by the generator can only stand and watch in wordless shock. Scotty has fainted, and although he had a camera ready, he did not take a single picture.

But Scotty does finally manage to send his story from the base radio, and his message, with which the film ends, adds a strange touch of fearful emotion to the close: "One of the world's greatest battles was fought and won today by the human race. Here on top of the world, a handful of American soldiers and civilians met the first invasion from another planet. . . . Now, before I bring you the details of the battle, I bring you a warning—to every

The creature bursts into the camp and is doused with inflammable fluid. But the flames do not prevent him from escaping.

one of you listening to the sound of my voice. Tell the world . . . tell this to everyone wherever they are: watch the skies . . . watch everywhere . . . keep looking . . . *watch the skies!*"

Not since the war years—when propaganda films routinely ended with warnings about insidious enemies in Europe and Asia poised to strike—had a

Tension mounts as Pat and his men set a new trap for the monster: a corridor wired to electrocute him (below). The alien enters. . . .

melodrama finished with such a deliberately realistic cautionary note. Hawks no doubt meant the ending not to be taken *too* seriously—intending, rather, a modern version of the *Dracula* epilogue in which Van Helsing warns the audience that "there *are* such things!" Howard Hawks had said he hoped his science fiction film would not be confused with the *Frankenstein* type of film, "an out-and-out horror thriller based on that which is impossible. The science-fiction film is based on that which is unknown but is given credibility by the use of scientific facts which parallel that which the viewer is asked to believe."

The Thing from Another World marked a milestone in intelligent, literate, realistic science fiction. Just as

Scotty gets his story through: "Tell the world . . . tell everyone . . . watch the skies!"

Hawks had predicted, it was an enormous financial success. But he was less than accurate in his prophecies regarding the science fiction film in general. Even though *The Thing* inspired imitations at other studios, it did not open "the vast new story markets" and push through the exploration of new, different plots that Hawks had envisioned. Instead, Hollywood soon went back to the "out-and-out horror thriller" of the old school—safer, cheaper, tried and true. This is why *The Thing from Another World* stands all the more isolated in the cinema of the fantastic.

TWENTY THOUSAND LEAGUES
UNDER THE SEA

Ned Land	Kirk Douglas
Captain Nemo	James Mason
Professor Aronnax	Paul Lukas
Conseil	Peter Lorre
The First Mate	Robert J. Wilke
John Howard	Carleton Young
Captain Farragut	Ted de Corsia
Diver	Percy Helton
Nemo's seal	Esmeralda

Produced by Walt Disney
Directed by Richard Fleischer
Based on the novel by Jules Verne
Screenplay by Earl Felton
Art director: John Meehan
Photography: Franz Lehy, Ralph Hammeras, Till Gabbani
Editor: Elmo Williams
Filmed in New Providence, Bahamas; Long Bay, Jamaica; Disney Studios
    in Burbank, California

Released by Buena Vista Productions December 14, 1954

Jules Verne died just three years after his fellow countryman Georges Méliès began his *Trip to the Moon*, a film largely based on Verne's own speculations. Verne had an enormous influence on Méliès and the pioneer film-makers working at the start of the twentieth century: they were all seized with the same visions, believing that his prophecies of the scientifically possible

235

were about to come true. And Verne's new age of technological marvels had a wide horizon. Not only did Méliès rocket to the moon, in 1907 he produced the first screen version of *Twenty Thousand Leagues Under the Sea*, the astonishing submarine adventure Verne had written in 1870. The author's scientific romances were perfect topics for the early film creators: dazzling forward looks at a new age ushering in fantastic inventions, one of which was the cinema itself, a scientific marvel already arrived.

Nine years later, Universal Studio released a second early version of *Twenty Thousand Leagues Under the Sea,* remarkable for 1916 in that it was the first narrative film in this country to use underwater photography, and remarkable also for its plot: it borrowed large chunks of Verne's

sequel novel of sorts, *Mysterious Island,* and even tacked on a fanciful new ending in which Captain Nemo leads an attack against a Sudan fort in which his daughter has been imprisoned.

But as the movies went into their next decades, Verne became largely neglected. Much of what he had prophesied had already come to pass. His stories seemed Victorian, antique. (A 1951 Columbia serial version of *Mysterious Island* thought it wise to add an interplanetary menace from Venus to the plight of the castaways on that island, and a 1961 big-budget feature version thought to include giant Ray Harryhausen crabs and bees.)

In 1954, however, Walt Disney, one of the great natural geniuses of the American film and one of the leading contributors to the cinema of fantasy, reached an important decision. The entire output of his studio had hitherto

A sea monster has been reported, and a ship with a cargo of gunpowder suddenly blows up (left). But nothing daunts brawling, boisterous seaman Ned Land.

been distributed by the RKO exchanges—which naturally enough took a good share of the profits—but from this point on Disney would distribute his films himself. However, he needed feature films in order to activate his new distribution company, named Buena Vista after the street on which he lived. Full-length cartoons were becoming increasingly costly and, in any event, took years to make. On the other hand, the live-action adaptations of children's classics that he had initiated, in 1950, with *Treasure Island* could be brought from planning board to theater screen faster and with less expense, and they were becoming increasingly popular. For his first release under the Buena Vista banner, and his first production in Cinemascope, he decided he wanted a very visual adventure story for family tastes, preferably based on an established classic known the world over. He chose *Twenty Thousand Leagues Under the Sea.*

Disney, who saw Verne as a colorful Victorian romantic, accentuated the period feeling of the story in order to present a gaslit science fictional fairyland, a parallel world to our real past where incredible, although piston-driven, futuristic machines are etched with filigree and laced with velvet plush. His film overlaid the numbing, impersonal scientific realities of today with the cozier, friendlier, less complex past, somehow sanctifying progress by showing the goodness of its roots. It struck an immediate response from the increasingly science-baffled, progress-weary audiences of the postatomic mid-fifties. It was, for the Disney organization, a triumph.

But everything was done to make it so; $250,000 was spent on sets alone out of a total budget of $5 million. Extensive underwater photography was done at Nassau in the Bahamas, where the ocean is clearest. For director,

Disney chose Richard Fleischer, then in his late thirties, who had made a name for himself directing such tight and gutsy little melodramas as *Armored Car Robbery* (1950) and *The Narrow Margin* (1952). (Ironically enough, Richard's father was the famed Max Fleischer, who headed a cartoon factory mildly competitive to Disney, producing such animated features as *Gulliver's Travels* [1939] and the classic *Superman* cartoon shorts of the early forties.) For the pivotal role of the brooding and introspective Captain Nemo, Disney picked James Mason, and the choice could not have been a happier one. Kirk Douglas was eager to play Ned Land, the hero, as it gave him a chance at a more lighthearted role than he had had for some time. In the key character parts of Professor Aronnax and Conseil, Disney cast Paul Lukas and Peter Lorre. Both actors had been out of Hollywood for some years, Lukas on the Broadway stage and Lorre directing in Europe. The Disney film would renew the screen careers of each, especially that of Lorre, who because of the film's success would make a specialty of character comedy roles.

Twenty Thousand Leagues Under the Sea begins with reports of a sea monster preying on American shipping lanes in the 1870s. Professor Aronnax of the National Museum of Paris and his assistant Conseil have come to San Francisco on the last lap of their journey to the Pacific to study the sea and its mysteries. They accept the invitation of the United States government to sail a warship into South Pacific waters, in order that the distinguished scientist could help confirm or deny the existence of a sea monster. Also on board is young harpooner Ned Land. Months pass, and the warship's captain is about to give up the search when, one night, a ship sighted on the horizon suddenly

At right, Ned and his friends Professor Aronnax (right) and Conseil (center) meet the strange Captain Nemo, and from his underwater ship they witness a sea burial.

explodes in a fearful flash. Obviously a cargo of gunpowder has gone up, sinking all hands, but what had the ship struck to set it off? Or, what had struck the ship? At once the monster is spotted in the waves: a fantastic finned creature with massive dark tail and eyes like flaming torches. As the warship fires its cannons—and Ned Land readies his harpoon—the great fish turns upon its new adversary and, accelerating to a terrible speed, rams the ship.

The jolt knocks Professor Aronnax and Conseil overboard, and to their horror the crippled warship limps away from them into the fog. Their fall has gone unnoticed, and they have been abandoned. For hours they float in the cold ocean waters, hanging on to a smashed piece of mast. Just when they have prepared to give up all hope, a strange metallic fin comes into view. It is the monster, which is actually a *ship!*

Aronnax and Conseil, full of wonder, climb down into the hull of the ship, which is below the surface of the water. The professor notes that the monster is quite able to *sink:* "There is great genius behind all this." Another visitor comes aboard—Ned Land, adrift in his small harpoon boat and also abandoned by the damaged warship. The three explore the incredible metal fish, its strange machinery and luxurious staterooms. In what appears to be the captain's cabin they peer through a large glass hull at the great vista of the ocean floor below . . . and see a group of men dressed in black rubbery suits conducting a burial service among the coral reefs.

The three try to escape, but after a fierce struggle they are captured and brought before the monster-ship's dark-bearded, saturnine Captain Nemo. He has heard of Aronnax and admired his writings, but Ned and Conseil cannot remain. "The sea has brought them, and the sea shall have them back." Aronnax protests (to which

240

As the ocean waters foam over our
friends' heads, Nemo decides not to
let them drown (upper left). Later,
in diving gear, they explore
underwater harvests, including
ancient treasure.

Nemo's face is a study in rage as he bombs another warship.

Nemo replies, "I am not what you call a civilized man, Professor") and ultimately insists upon sharing his companions' fate. The three are placed on deck as the ship begins to submerge. As the ocean waters rise over their heads, Nemo has a change of heart resurfaces, and brings them back aboard.

That night, they dine with Nemo on strange foods, all harvested from the sea. They learn that the ship is called the *Nautilus,* and they themselves are on a curious probation: not actually prisoners, but not quite guests, as the *Nautilus* tolerates neither. For the moment, however, they face a fantastic voyage of discovery. Aronnax is especially fascinated by Nemo's hunts and harvests at the bottom of the sea, his "rule over this forgotten reach of Nature"—while Ned is astonished to learn that the *Nautilus* uses gold and precious jewels recovered from sunken galleons as ballast.

Although fierce storms lash the ocean's surface, the submarine cruises under the turbulence serenely undisturbed, while Nemo plays wildly on the great organ in his ornate salon. As time goes on, Nemo seems determined to show Aronnax everything about the working of the ship, including his source of power, a blinding pulsing mass behind thick protective metal shields. "It was apparent," notes the professor to himself, "that Nemo had discovered what mankind has always sought: the veritable dynamic power of the universe!" (The addition of atomic power to the *Nautilus* was a Disney inspiration. Coincidentally, no doubt, the United States' own atomic submarine *Nautilus* was launched the same year the film was released.)

Aronnax studies the strange, moody captain with increasing interest. Nemo has deliberately cut himself off from the upper world. "On the surface there is hunger and fear. Men exercise unjust laws. They fight . . . tear one another to pieces. And only a few feet under the waves their reign ceases, their evil drowns. Here, on the ocean floor, is the only independence. Here, I am free."

One day, an island is sighted, and the professor finds another clue to the forces in conflict within Nemo. Aronnax joins a secret landing party—Nemo explains this is a prison island, "the white man's grave"—and through a spyglass watches chained, whipped men carrying sacks of nitrate and phosphate for ammunition, "the seeds of war," aboard a ship that flies no flag. Nemo suddenly confesses to Aronnax, "I was once one of those pitiful wretches." That evening, as the ammunition ship steams out of the bay, the submarine accelerates once more. There are several shattering explosions, and the ammunition ship sinks in minutes. Nemo has destroyed it.

The professor and Ned are appalled that none of the seamen aboard the doomed vessel was allowed to escape, but Nemo turns on them furiously. "They are the assassins, the dealers in death; I am the avenger!" With an agonized cry of despair, Nemo denounces the unnamed nation that took everything away from him except the awesome secret of his power, tortured him, murdered his wife and son, placed him on that prison island. "Do you know the meaning of love, Professor? What you fail to understand is the power of *hate.* It can fill the heart as well as love can." A bitter substitute, Aronnax remarks, as he leaves.

Although Ned had promised the professor from the beginning that he would do nothing to disturb the delicate balance of Nemo's hospitality, he now actively plans to escape. He begins to throw bottles containing messages overboard at every opportunity. When the *Nautilus* docks

Cannibals converge on the *Nautilus* and attempt to board her (above). They are scattered by electricity, but Nemo is furious with Ned (right).

briefly off the coast of New Guinea, Ned begs for the opportunity to visit the beach. Nemo grimly consents but warns him not to go farther inland than the coast, for it is cannibal territory, and "they eat liars with the same enthusiasm they eat honest men." Naturally, as soon as Ned hits shore he follows a trail into the interior through a beautiful tropical forest. Suddenly,

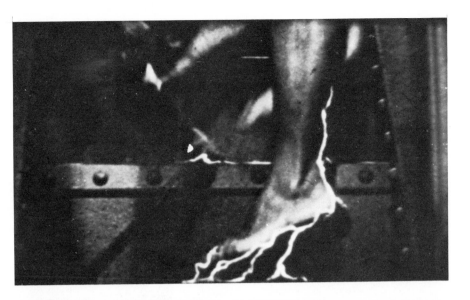

however, he spies several human skulls on posts blocking his path. He turns and runs, with hundreds of angry natives hard behind him, hurling spears. He barely makes it to the submarine in time. The natives follow in outrigger canoes and clamber into the *Nautilus*'s deck. How can they be stopped from boarding her? Nemo pulls a switch, and harmless charges of electricity shock and scatter the natives, who then head quickly on their canoes for the safety of their own world.

Nemo is furious with Ned for disobeying him, but before he can mete out punishment a warship is sighted. When the *Nautilus* rams the ship, it is severely damaged by cannon fire and forced to submerge to the ocean floor, where it faces a deadly enemy making a

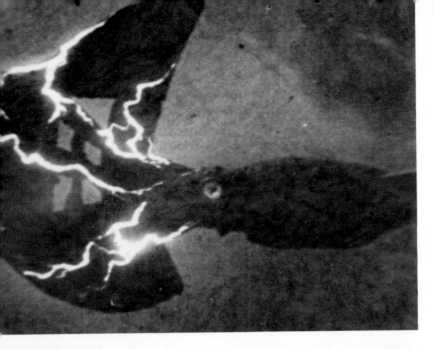

From the ocean's floor, a gigantic squid attacks the ship (above). Nemo himself, spear in hand, makes for the creature's eyes. When he fails, Ned's harpoon lands true; he saves the life of Captain Nemo.

sudden surprise attack: a giant squid!

In a domain where man has never been before, Nemo's crew battles a sea creature whose tentacles are almost as long as the *Nautilus* itself and are now wrapped around the ship in a death grip. All the *Nautilus*'s defensive devices seem useless against the beast. Their only chance of winning is to fight at close quarters, "hand to hand."

Nemo gives the order to surface, and

246

he steps out with his men onto the deck in a stormy, swirling sea, as tangled tentacles snake toward them. "The only vital spot is between the eyes," Nemo shouts as, spear in hand, he dodges the groping coils to make for the evil head-sac with its snapping beak. His spear misses its mark, and a tentacle pulls him into the churning ocean. But Ned's harpoon *does* land true. A moment later Ned jumps into the sea

and pulls the dazed Nemo back on deck. "You have saved my life," mutters Nemo, weakly. It is the first time he has shown gratitude.

In the next few days Nemo's dark mood changes. He confesses to Aronnax that he had planned to use the professor as an emissary to the outside world, to give the world the secret of his power—can it be atomic?—if nations would only lay down their arms,

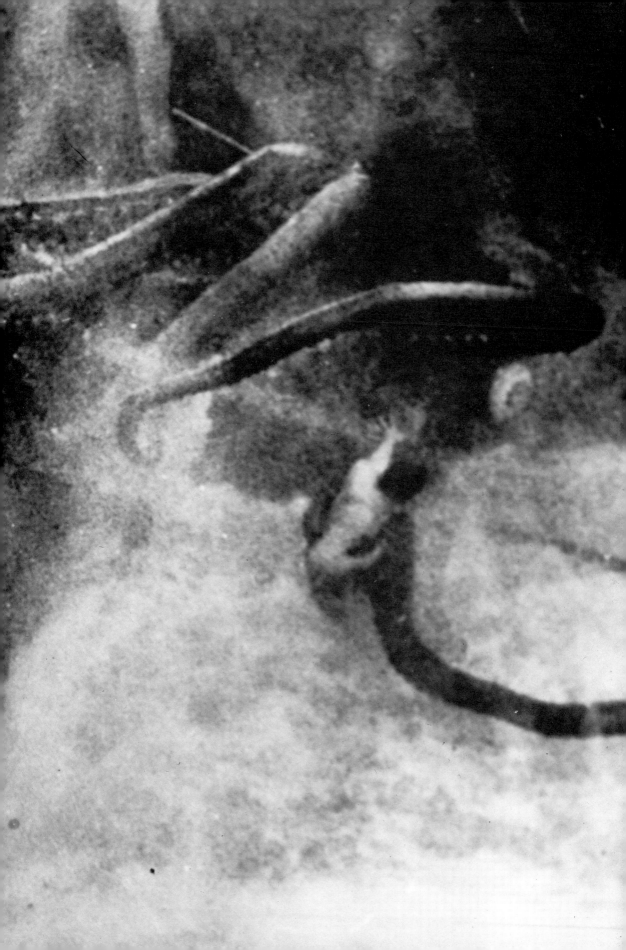

abolish their slave camps, and end war.
"I will give mankind enough energy to
lift it out of the depths of Hell into
Heaven—or destroy it."

But when the *Nautilus* docks at
Nemo's secret island retreat, Vulcania,
an armada of warships awaits it. Ned's
bottles carrying messages giving the
Nautilus's continuing course have been
picked up. There is a gun battle, and
Nemo is seriously wounded. He is
carried back to the submarine by his
men.

"I am dying . . . and the *Nautilus* is
dying with me. In a matter of minutes
an explosion such as the world has
never known will destroy my island and
all its works forever." He orders the
ship brought down for the last time to
its final deep resting-place under the sea.

But Ned is not willing to die with the
Nautilus. Knocking out his guard, he
carries Aronnax and Conseil out of the
submarine just before it submerges, and
the three cast off in a skiff, again at the
mercy of the open sea as they had been
at the beginning of their adventure.
There is an incredible explosion, and
another; the entire terrain of Vulcania,
with the warships in its harbor, is
obliterated in flame—and a giant
mushroom cloud rises above the
horizon. As the castaways watch, the
Nautilus rolls on its side; its nose
suddenly points heavenward, and the
submarine lurches beneath the waves.
And we hear an echo of Captain
Nemo's dying words: "There is
hope. . . . When the world is ready for a
new and better life, all this will
someday come to pass . . . in God's
good time. . . ."

*Twenty Thousand Leagues Under
the Sea* pioneered two themes that
were not to become fully popular with
audiences until years after: the intense,
militant pacifism of Captain Nemo, and
his conservation activities on the
ocean's floor. Disney's film was really

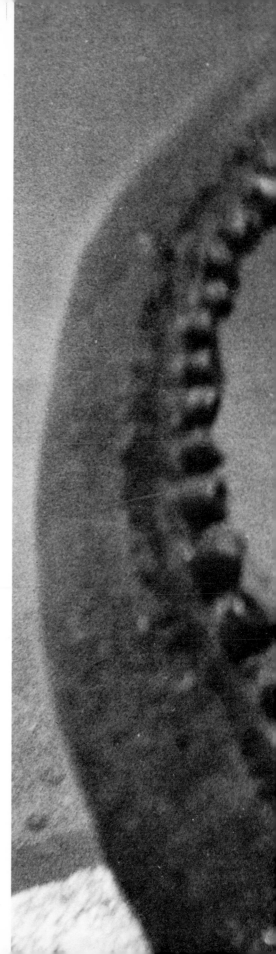

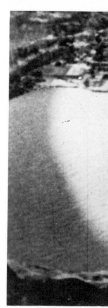

the first popular effort to show the ocean's awesome beauty, its secrets, and the possible benefits coming from it to mankind. With Nemo we were entering an unreal, fantastic world, yet a world, however strange and timeless, that possesses a sense of actuality and in which people are concerned with the very same matters that concern us. And it is a world of immense riches, which, as Nemo had demonstrated, could be conquered. It was this excitement, and this charm, that went far toward making *Twenty Thousand Leagues Under the Sea* a classic adventure film of the fantastic. (A television special on the film's underwater photography won Disney an Emmy Award from the National Academy of Television Arts and Sciences.)

The film also sparked a far-reaching revival of interest in the works of Jules Verne as cinematic material. At least half a dozen major motion pictures were made in the next decade from his other prophetic novels, ranging in themes from *Around the World in Eighty Days* (1956) to *From the Earth to the Moon* (1958) to *Journey to the Center of the Earth* (1959). Disney's very dramatic and intelligent characterization of Captain Nemo—and

The *Nautilus* docks at Nemo's secret island, only to find soldiers and warships awaiting it. Nemo, wounded, pulls the switch. . . .

252

"An explosion such as the world has never known will destroy my island and all its works forever."

James Mason's superb portrayal of him—gave that Verne figure legendary status. Nemo survives the blast at Vulcania and is allowed to find his final harbor at *Mysterious Island,* and in this Charles Schneer film Nemo is played by Herbert Lom. Later, in the MGM production of *Captain Nemo's Underwater City* (1970)—which presupposes the captain and his crew have the power to build a vast domed city of gold at the bottom of the sea— he is played by Robert Ryan. Being virtual emperor of this undersea domain makes him no less the Nemo of old, rescuing castaways on the ocean's surface and muttering against munitions kings.

The dynamism of the tortured Captain Nemo and the mysteries of his underwater world combine to make *Twenty Thousand Leagues Under the Sea* a fantastic exploration not only of an unfamiliar ocean universe, but also of the depths of a strange and fascinating human being. As further evidence of the durability of the saga, *Nautilus* rides in both California's Disneyland and Florida's Disney World are the most popular attractions of both amusement parks—making the Disney organization the owner of the eighth largest submarine fleet in the world!

INVASION OF THE BODY SNATCHERS

Dr. Miles Bennell	Kevin McCarthy
Becky Driscoll	Dana Wynter
Dr. Dan Kaufman	Larry Gates
Theodora Velichec	Carolyn Jones
Jack Velichec	King Donovan
Nick Grivett	Ralph Dumke
Sally	Jean Willes
Wilma Lentz	Virginia Christine
Ira Lentz	Tom Fadden
Grandma Grimaldi	Beatrice Maude
Jimmy Grimaldi	Bobby Clark
Charlie Buckholtz	Sam Peckinpah
Dr. Harvey Bassett	Richard Deacon
Dr. Hill	Whit Bissell

Drected by Don Siegel
Produced by Walter Wanger
Screenplay by Daniel Geoffrey Homes Mainwaring
From the novel by Jack Finney
Music: Carmen Dragon
Director of Photography: Ellsworth Fredericks, ASC

Released by Allied Artists May 1, 1956

At the start of the fifties, with the release of *The Thing,* the cinema of the fantastic looked as if it were entering a promising vogue of intelligent film-making. By the mid-fifties, the vogue still lingered, but all intelligence was gone. Science fiction and horror themes were being explored in only routine ways. Inspired in large part by *The Thing,* the invasion of earth and the rape of civilization seemed the concern of the fantasy film throughout the decade. Generally the menace was something such as a prehistoric creature revived by an ecological disturbance. The formula was constant: a terrible menace strikes first at some remote locality, then swings in to crash through a large city, where it is ultimately destroyed by a union of science and the military. Endless variants on this plot were churned out by both the major studios and the independents.

In 1956 Allied Artists released *Invasion of the Body Snatchers* as one of several low-budget features in the science fiction and horror category. They were doing no more than making their contribution to the "invasion" trend; they had no idea what an extraordinary hit they had on their hands. Their expectations for it were no more than average. But its producer, Walter Wanger, who had selected the Jack Finney serial from the pages of *Collier's,* had higher hopes for it and fashioned it with love and care.

As director he selected the talented Don Siegel, who had risen from being an editor and montage-constructor at Warner Brothers to directing tough, tight little thrillers. Wanger had worked with him two years before, on *Riot in Cell Block Eleven,* and knew he was expert in creating claustrophobic tensions. For his leads, Wanger chose two players able, above all else, to deliver lines intelligently. Kevin McCarthy had started his career on the New York stage, and his movie debut (in 1952) was in the adaptation of Broadway's *Death of a Salesman.* Dana Wynter, a British import noted for her portrayal of patrician beauties, was cast here as the cool and competent divorcée heroine. Wanger wanted *his* invasion of alien forces not to happen

at some remote outpost, peopled by superheroic stereotypes in uniform, but to erupt into the middle of the lives of ordinary yet thinking people.

Although the stories are quite different, there are resemblances between *Invasion of the Body Snatchers* and *The Thing.* Each deals with an alien attempt to colonize Earth, and in each the method is the spreading of seeds or spores. In each the human protagonists are realistically, carefully drawn, and the dialogue is written with a sharp ear for the way people actually speak (in both it sometimes overlaps). But the earlier film had a central menace—the Thing itself—which is to be destroyed; in *Invasion of the Body Snatchers* the menace is not nearly so clear and present. No one knows where the seeds come from, or at what point they impregnated the soil of Earth and started growing. The menace is, in a particularly apt phrase, faceless. One cannot destroy the alien invader and have done with it; the invader is everywhere, assuming our shapes, moving among us, conquering us by consuming us, in some sort of interplanetary miscegenation where our enemies are ourselves. Watching the movie, we can feel a fear, almost a kind of paranoia, generating almost more anxiety than the terminal warning of *The Thing,* which cautions us to watch the skies. In *Invasion of the Body Snatchers* our fears force us to watch one another.

The film starts dramatically. Dr. Hill of the State Mental Hospital Board has been brought, in a police car screaming through the night, to examine a young doctor who has just arrived at the emergency hospital in a dangerous emotional state. The patient, forcibly restrained, begs someone to hear his story. It began, for him, just a week ago. He is young Miles Bennell,

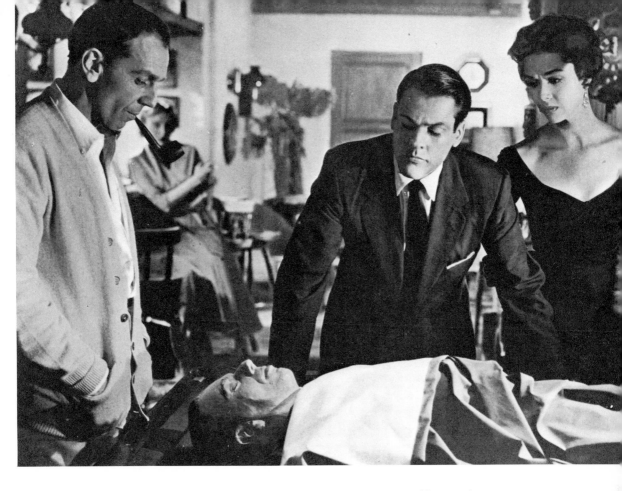

Jack shows Dr. Miles Bennell the body he has found. Its face is a duplicate of his own!

practicing in the small California town of Santa Mira. He has just been recalled from a medical convention by his nurse, worried over what seems to be an epidemic of patients. As he steps from the train at the Santa Mira station, everything appears to be sunny, peaceful, untroubled. And yet . . .

None of the ailing patients turns up. Looking out of his office window, Miles sees some of them in the street, moving about their everyday affairs, apparently recovered. He also spots an old romance, Becky Driscoll. Becky had married another and emigrated to England to live; she has now returned, divorced. She stops by his office on a professional matter: her cousin Wilma seems strangely convinced that the

uncle with whom she lives has turned imposter, that he is someone else. "But that's ridiculous," Miles says. There are, however, other cases. A young boy screams that his mother is not his mother. From the town's only psychiatrist, Dan Kaufman, Miles learns there have been dozens of similar complaints. An odd neurosis. "Worry about what's happening in the world, probably."

And then Miles, having dinner in a restaurant with Becky, receives an emergency call from an old friend, Jack Velichec, a writer. They rush to his home, and Jack shows him an incredible sight. Lying on a billiard table is a body. A body with Jack's face. And yet it is not a dead man. It

257

has no fingerprints, and the features are indistinct—*unfinished.* "I wonder if there's any connection," Miles muses. "There's something strange going on in Santa Mira. . . ." Jack's wife, Teddy, is very uneasy, and Jack too is nervous—he cuts his hand making a drink. Miles, unsure what will happen next, asks Jack to sit up that night watching the body. Meantime, he must get Becky home.

Miles drives Becky home and makes sure she gets inside. As they part, Becky's father comes up from the basement. For a moment, Miles notices something odd about the man. But he shrugs it off. Returning to his own home, he finds Jack and Teddy there,

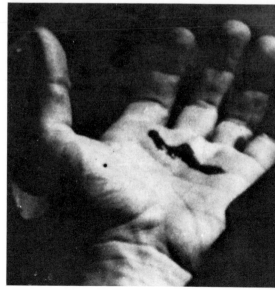

258

In the greenhouse Miles and his friends watch the immense seed pods open—within the milky sap they see bodies forming—and destroy them. One resembles Miles. Previously, Jack's pod double had even managed to duplicate the fresh cut on his hand.

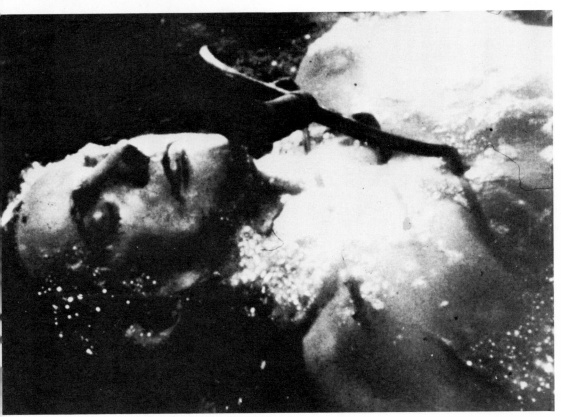

both hysterical. The body on the
billiard table is coming alive. Jack's
features are filling in! Even to the fresh
cut on his hand. Miles gives Teddy a
shot of whiskey and telephones Dan
Kaufman to come. Then a sudden fear
stabs him. Is Becky in danger? Acting
on impulse, he drives to the Driscoll
house. Opening a basement window, he
lets himself into the cellar. In a bin he
finds another body, a double for
Becky!

Quickly making his way to Becky's
bedroom, he carries her, still asleep,
from the house. . . .

Psychiatrist Dan Kaufman is
incredulous. "I want to see one of these
things." Jack takes Miles and Dan back
to his house, where they discover that
the thing is now gone from the billiard

table. Kaufman makes little of it. There's a mystery, yes, but not a supernatural one. A corpse had been dumped in the Velichec home, then removed. The facial muscles were relaxed by death, and the corpse appeared featureless. The fingerprints had been burned away by acid. As for the body Miles saw—a hallucination. But Miles refuses to accept this pat rationalization. And so they make their way to the Driscoll cellar.

Becky's double is gone as well; only a clutter of rags lies in the bin. "Your mind has been playing tricks with you," Kaufman says humorously to Miles. The lights go on suddenly, and Becky's father descends the stairs, carrying a shotgun. He appears perplexed, but entirely normal. He had

Becky's father interrupts Dan Kaufman's theorizing (left). Miles finds a body in the cellar (above). As Miles and Becky go for help, they have spotted a gas station attendant putting something in the trunk of their car: two pods. Now Miles burns them.

thought he heard prowlers and has just called the police. As Kaufman attempts to explain what has happened—and to make light of it—Nick, the middle-aged Santa Mira chief of police, arrives. A corpse with its fingerprints removed has been found in a burning haystack outside town. This seems to explain what happened to the body that had been in Jack's house. "All right, break it up," Nick orders. "Go on home."

Miles is still uneasy the next day, though all his patients appear recovered, even Wilma and the young boy who had turned against his mother. That night he and Becky are invited to the Velichecs for steaks on the outdoor barbecue. There is a greenhouse in the backyard, and from it Miles hears a faint popping noise. He steps inside. Under the soil tables are what look like *immense seed pods.* Each of them is bursting open, with a gush of milky sap, to reveal a quivering fetuslike thing inside. Miles screams. All agree, this is where the doppelgänger bodies have come from, from these fantastic seed pods, which then grow into our shapes. "But when they're finished, what happens to *our* bodies?" Becky wails. "I don't know. . . ." Miles thinks for a minute. "They must take over when we're asleep. And then the original body is removed—or disintegrated." Suddenly he realizes that it's happened already to a lot of his patients. To Wilma. To Becky's father. Nick and Dan Kaufman—they've been taken over too. People must be warned. He tries to reach the Federal Bureau of Investigation in Los Angeles, but the call will not go through. "That office is open day and night!" He realizes the extent of the forces against him.

Where do these seeds come from? Becky asks. Miles shakes his head. "So much has been discovered in the last few years—anything is possible." The things must be tremendously powerful. "All that body in your cellar needed

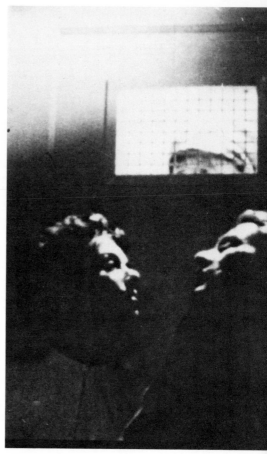

Miles and Becky hide from the friends they know have been "taken over" (left). Miles manages to overcome Kaufman and Jack with a sedative.

was a mind, and it was taking yours while you were asleep." Miles stabs at the pods in the greenhouse with a pitchfork and sends Jack and Teddy for help to the next town. Because he cannot place a call to an FBI office through the Santa Mira telephone system, he and Becky drive to a gas station in the hope that a pay booth might still be unaffected. But it is useless. And while they try the phone they spot the gas station attendants, a husband and wife who are old friends of Miles, putting something in the trunk of their car. Stopping a short ways from the station, they open the trunk. Inside are two fresh, gleaming pods. Miles removes them, sets them

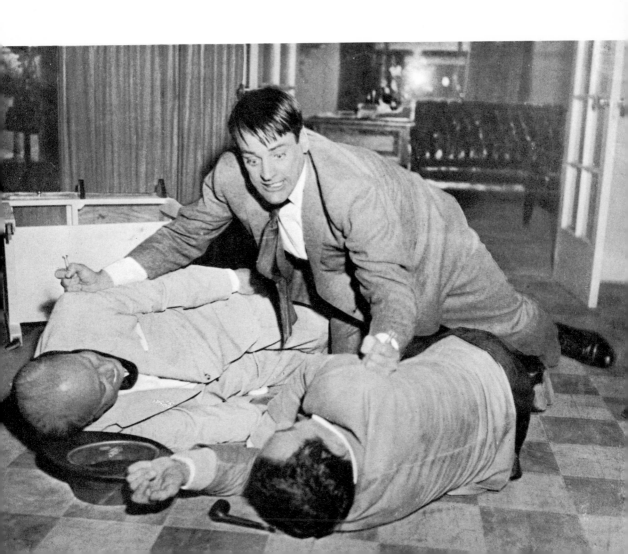

ablaze with an ignited car flare, and drives off.

There is no one they can contact. They see Miles's nurse through a window of her house fondling one of the pods and giving instructions about them to her neighbors, as matter-of-factly as if she were conducting a class in first aid. All of Santa Mira's police force seems changed, and over a car radio Miles and Becky hear orders for their capture. They hide in Miles's office until morning. "We can't close our eyes all night, or we might wake up—*changed.*" Miles looks at Becky soberly. "In my practice I've seen how people have allowed their humanity to drain away . . . slowly, instead of all at once. They didn't seem to mind. . . . All of us. We harden our hearts. Grow callous. Only when we have to fight to stay human we realize how precious it is."

Dawn brightens Santa Mira's town square under Miles's office window, and it is just like any other Saturday morning. Except that it seems busier. People are converging on the square, and farmers' trucks from the outlying districts drive up. Nick, the chief of police, steps into the middle of the square with a megaphone. "Crescent City. All of you with relatives in Crescent City, go to Truck One." *The trucks are filled with seed pods.* The crowds remove the pods, as Nick mentions other nearby towns. Miles watches from his window, horrified. "It's like a malignant disease—being spread throughout the countryside!" He hears Jack's voice outside his office door. *Thank God! He's brought help!* But the Jack who steps through the door is one of them.

"Don't fight it, Miles. You've got to go to sleep sometime." Dan Kaufman is with Jack, and tries to reason with Miles. Think of the marvelous thing that has happened. Seeds drifting through space for years,

out of the sky, took root by chance in a farmer's field—to offer us an untroubled world. "No love, no emotion . . ." By tomorrow, Miles will be one of them. "Love, desire, ambition, faith—without them, life is so simple."

But Miles will not yet concede defeat to this new world. A hypodermic needle in each hand, he manages to inject both Jack and Kaufman with a sedative, and they collapse. He pulls at Becky, shouting, "Our only hope is the highway." They make their way out into the street, trying to imitate the others in the street by walking slowly, their expressions blank. But Becky screams when a dog is nearly hit by a farmer's truck, and a traffic cop eyes them suspiciously.

Moments later the town's main siren sounds, and Miles realizes all is lost. They start to run. A mob begins to follow them, an incredible mob of seemingly ordinary townsmen, gathering momentum through the streets. Miles and Becky lose their pursuers in the hills outside Santa Mira and take refuge in an old mine passage. They hear music: people singing. Human voices. While Miles goes to investigate, Becky sinks to her knees, exhausted. Exiting from the mine, Miles discovers in the valley spread beneath him endless greenhouses harvesting the pods. The singing voices are merely from a radio on one of the trucks being loaded. He returns to the safety of the mine cave to discover a changed Becky. He kisses her, and there is only a passive response. "I went to sleep, Miles, and it happened. Stop acting like a fool and accept us." Miles backs away in horror. *"He's in here,"* Becky screams, alerting the others to Miles's presence. *"He's in here!"*

Miles runs, cold fear gripping him. Behind him he hears others following him. His only hope is to get to the highway. He stumbles in the darkness

They try to appear like the others, but soon Miles and Becky must run—and the populace of Santa Mira pursues them. . . .

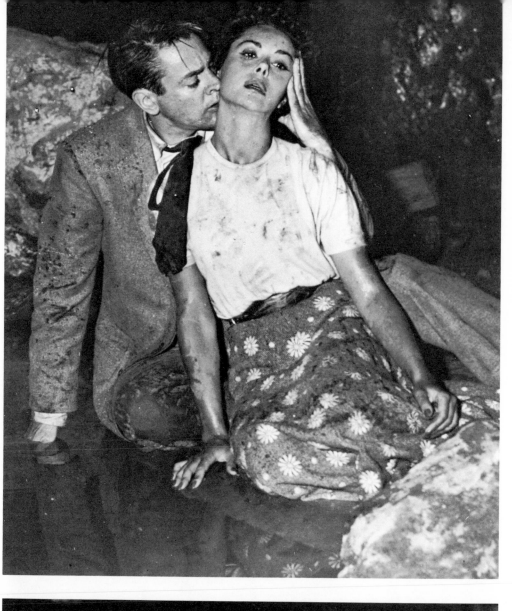

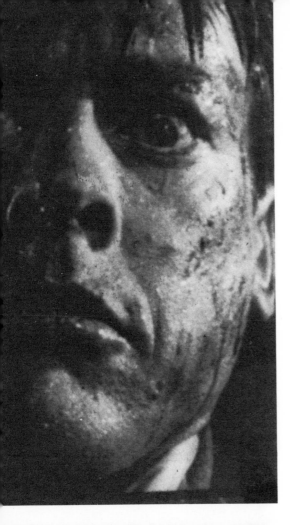

down through shrub and underbrush onto the valley floor, until ahead of him he sees the ribbons of light of the highway itself. It is crowded with traffic. Miles hurls himself between the cars, begging someone, anyone, to stop. *"Listen to me, to me, we're being invaded; you're in danger. . . ."* A truck lumbers by, labeled "Los Angeles—San Francisco"; Miles hoists himself up onto the back of it, if only to make some distance between himself and his pursuers by the side of the road. *Inside the truck is a massive consignment of seed pods.* Miles falls from his perch and is nearly run down by the car behind. He runs blindly between the lanes of traffic, headlights glaring into his face, as in an incredible climax the camera pushes into his agonized features. *"You're in danger! They're here already! You're next! You're next! You're next . . . !"*

At one point the plan was to end *Invasion of the Body Snatchers* at this terrifying moment, perhaps one of the most terrifying in the history of the screen. But a framing narrative was ultimately constructed in order to provide what the studio felt was a more positive ending, one in which our side could win out. Picked up on the highway by the state police, Miles is thought insane but is allowed to tell his story to Dr. Hill of the State Mental

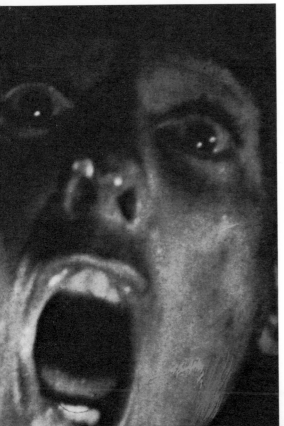

In the safety of an abandoned mine, Miles kisses Becky . . . and realizes with horror she has become one of them. He screams.

267

Miles darts into a traffic-choked highway in the film's great climax: "Listen to me, we're being invaded; you're in danger. . . ."

Hospital. The latter is distrustful at first but chances to overhear two other doctors discussing an overturned truck filled with an odd cargo: giant seed pods. With commendable alacrity Hill jumps into action. "Call the FBI! Blockade all highways leading out of Santa Mira. . . ." The invaders will not conquer without a struggle.

Invasion of the Body Snatchers has a few weaknesses. The early acceptance by Jack and Miles of the body on the billiard table seems on repeated viewings rather unquestioning. They arrive at their theories of interplanetary invasion rather swiftly and surefootedly. But these minor carpings aside, the film is an intensely realistic drama of everyday people defending everyday values against inhuman invasion, done with a great deal of human feeling. Indeed it is the humanity of the drama that is its greatest strength, and it is this, too, that makes the story play so well. Miles tells us that the lessening of human interchange in this complicated world, the hardening and callousness, may have given the alien seed a chance to sprout. No similar theory is thought of in *The Thing,* for instance, where the menace is impervious to all emotional climates. Yet Miles clearly hints, in a film whose ending is quite as propagandistic as the climax of *The Thing,* that only when human love and feeling drain away can the body snatchers actually take over. It is a message for us to carry.

FORBIDDEN PLANET

Dr. Morbius	Walter Pidgeon
Altaira	Anne Francis
Commander Adams	Leslie Nielsen
Lieutenant "Doc" Ostrow	Warren Stevens
Chief Quinn	Richard Anderson
Cook	Earl Holliman
Lieutenant Farman	Jack Kelly
Bosun	George Wallace
and	
Robby the Robot	

Directed by Fred McLeod Wilcox
Produced by Nicholas Nayfack
Screenplay by Cyril Hume
Based on a story by Irving Block and Allen Adler
Electronic tonalities by Louis and Bebe Barron
Special effects by A. Arnold Gillespie, Warren Newcombe, Irving G. Ries,
      and Joshua Meador (through courtesy of Walt Disney Productions)
Director of Photography: George J. Folsey, ASC

Released (in CinemaScope and Eastman color) by MGM August 1, 1956

By the nineteen fifties, in films like *The Thing,* the cinema of the fantastic had begun to concentrate on interplanetary invasion. With *Invasion of the Body Snatchers,* the alien enemy became intent upon our very minds and souls. A month later, in that same year of 1956, Metro-Goldwyn-Mayer studios released what it hoped was the ultimate in big-budget, "class" science fiction, a handsome and colorful epic in which the enemy *was* our own minds and souls.

Forbidden Planet, a project MGM had begun several years earlier, was a

We have begun the exploration, conquest, and colonization of deep space (above). The crew of Planets Cruiser C57D studies its destination on the viewing screen: an Earth-type world called Altair IV (right). The ship lands (below).

deliberate attempt to create a science fiction A production. (Twelve years later MGM would try again—with *2001.*) An extremely intelligent script was fashioned by veteran science fiction writer Cyril Hume from an original story by Irving Block and Allen Adler. The story had deliberate parallels with Shakespeare's *The Tempest:* the island is now a forbidding planet where Walter Pidgeon, a brooding scientist, lives in isolation, much like the magician Prospero, with his daughter and his "Ariel," a spirited but devoted robot

All scenes in the film are set either on the Forbidden Planet or on the spaceship approaching it; there are no sequences at all on our familiar Earth. While some of the planet's terrain remains undeveloped backdrop, a high order of imagination went into the creation of its civilization and the instruments by which the film's

extraordinary Caliban begins his destructive forces. Even though *Forbidden Planet* can be appreciated solely as gorgeous, brightly colored space opera, polished with the loving hands of MGM's superior design and effects people and enacted by handsome young contract players portraying the astronauts of a century from now, it is much more complex. The film's philosophy seems in large part a muted replay of *The Thing*'s basic conflict between science and the military, except that the pilots are far more receptive to science's special ways. They, too, thirst for knowledge: when the enemy appears they seek to understand as well as to contain it. And when they finally *do* understand the enemy's secret, and what has unleashed it, the revelation is so astonishing and innovative that it has widened the conventions of the science fiction screen. And the cinematic science fiction and fantasy screen was not to widen its horizons again until *2001*, more than a decade later. *Forbidden Planet* truly achieves a bold new cinematic plateau.

When the film opens in the last decade of the twenty-first century, men—surprisingly—have only just landed on the moon. By A.D. 2200, however, we have reached the other planets of our solar system and—aided by the development of hyper-drive, which enables our rockets to travel faster than the speed of light—we have begun the exploration, conquest, and colonization of deep space. We watch as the huge, gleaming, saucer-shaped United Planets Cruiser C57D hurtles across the galaxy, a year's journey from Earth, on a special mission to the planetary system of the great main-sequence star Altair. It is to land on the fourth planet circling this sun—an "Earth-type" planet—to search for survivors of a party of prospecting scientists who landed there twenty

years before and from whom nothing has been heard since. As the circular cruiser spins across the face of the green and seemingly uninhabited planet—viewed by the vigilant Commander Adams (Leslie Nielsen) and the officers of his crew (Warren Stevens, Jack Kelly, and Richard Anderson)—we become increasingly aware of the rich, atonal score of electronic music composed for the film by Louis and Bebe Barron, the first such electronic score ever created for a feature film. Its unearthly, celestial sounds closely suit both the soaring wonder and, later, rising terror of the Forbidden Planet.

As Commander Adams prepares to land, instruments tell him his ship is being radar-scanned. The ship's radio picks up a voice that identifies itself as Dr. Morbius, one of the scientists of the original expedition. He hardly welcomes them, but, instead, urges them to turn back: "I cannot assume responsibility for the safety of your crew." Puzzled, defiant, Adams charts his course for a landing. As a precaution, he orders all crew members to carry sidearms.

The cruiser descends upon a pleasant, red-soiled desert flat, with strange rock formations strutting into a green sky and enormous sun. In the distance, a cloud of dust hurtles toward them like a bullet. It is a robot—human in size, its domed computer head twitching in a frenzy of clicking and blinking. It is driving a three-passenger dunemobile. He is here to take them to the residence, the robot states. "If you do not speak English, I am at your disposal with 187 other languages along with their various dialects and sub-tongues." The robot is monitored to respond to the name "Robby."

Suspiciously, Adams and his two lieutenants, "Doc" Ostrow and Jerry Farman, board the vehicle. At once they are transported to a comfortable

The crew step out for their first
view of Altair IV. The first creature
they encounter is a robot, driving
its own transport vehicle.

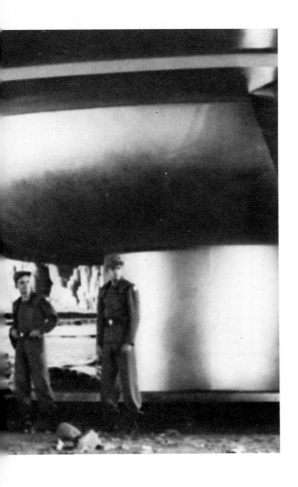

ranch-style abode, where they are greeted by the bearded, saturnine Morbius pleasantly enough, but with pointed reference to their disturbance of his privacy. He invites them to lunch, a lunch served by Robby and even prepared by him from synthetics. The robot is a creature of "absolutely selfless obedience." However, he has built-in robotic limitations: if ordered to injure a rational being—that is, man—his components would start fusing until he had blown every circuit in his body!

Commander Adams is puzzled at the absence of any other members of the expedition. Morbius explains: in the first year, one by one, they succumbed to "a planetary force here . . . some dark, terrible, incomprehensible force." Only Morbius and his wife were immune because of their "special love for this new world." She died a few months after the others, but of natural causes. The scientists, however, died by being literally torn apart, limb from limb, by an invisible force, which in the nineteen years since has never again manifested itself to Morbius.

Suddenly a beautiful young girl enters the room—Altaira, Morbius's daughter. The scientist is visibly displeased; he had wanted her to remain in her room until the visitors had departed. But Altaira has never before seen a man or any human being other than her father, and she could not be kept away. The young officers, having spent the last year in hyper-space, are enchanted.

Even though Cruiser C57D is technically on a rescue mission, Morbius refuses to be transported back to Earth. His work is on Altair IV; he cannot spare the two years it would take to bring him to Earth and back. The scientist urges Adams and his crew to quit the planet immediately, but the commander must radio Earth for his instructions. The ship's transmitters are

273

For Altaira, who had never before seen a man,
romance begins (above). There is horseplay at
the ship's base (below), but Commander
Adams is uneasy.

malfunctioning; they will take a few days to repair. Morbius anxiously allows his visitors to use Robby's special powers to hasten the job's completion.

While the work is going on, all the officers pay a good deal of attention to Altaira, and she to them. Lieutenant Farman even gives the girl a biology lesson in kissing. When Altaira in all innocence tells Morbius of this, he is furious.

That night an invisible being enters the giand cruiser, past two guards who notice nothing, breaks through a heavy metal hatch, and smashes vital equipment. Earth can no longer be contacted.

Adams can only think that Morbius has had something to do with this sabotage. He confronts the scientist, and the latter angrily agrees the time has come for clarification. "In times long past this planet was the home of a mighty and noble race of beings which called themselves the Krel," begins Morbius, setting the stage for the most intellectually exciting and stimulating section of the film: the archaeology of the Krel.

This race was a million years ahead of human morality and technology; they had conquered even their baser selves, abolishing sickness and crime and all injustice. "Then, seemingly on the threshold of some supreme accomplishment, which was to crown their entire history, this all but divine race perished in a single night." Since that terrible extinction two thousand centuries ago, there has been no Krel civilization above the surface of Altair IV. But Morbius takes Adams and one of his lieutenants—the young ship's physician, "Doc" Ostrow—on a breathtaking tour of what remains of the subterranean world of the Krel.

First, they visit a gleaming laboratory, its circuits flashing and dimming. It is here that, for twenty years, Morbius has tried to pierce the Krel's alphabet, logic, and science. Morbius, demonstrating a headpiece that can translate the user's thoughts into momentarily living three-dimensional forms, reveals that the stimulus of this and other of the lab's instruments has permanently doubled the intellectual capacity of his brain. He also reveals that in the days before their final annihilation the Krel had been devoting their entire energies to a project that they hoped would free them from physical instrumentality, catapulting them beyond the confines of matter. Was it this project that destroyed them? Adams wonders.

He marvels at the awesome power of the laboratory itself, still operating after two thousand centuries. Morbius agrees the power *is* incredible: in the lab are panel after panel of gauges, each one calibrating ten times the power of the one preceding it—power multiplied almost infinitely! And then Morbius takes the two spacemen to the source of the power . . . in a shuttle car that hurtles them deep into the bowels of the planet. "Prepare your minds for a new scale of physical scientific values, gentlemen."

They are in a shaft so enormous it would dwarf the Grand Canyon. They are on one of 7,800 levels going down forty miles; around them is the noisy roar of circuits constantly breaking; the machinery never rests. The planet is riddled by four hundred similar shafts. And all this time the power dynamos, with all their unimaginable harnessed power, have been patiently waiting, lubricating themselves, replacing spare parts . . . waiting . . .

That night, although electronic safeguards have been placed around the cruiser since the sabotage, something again breaks through: an unseen something that leaves deep marks in the ground, that depresses the heavy steel rungs leading to the ship's entrance.

The chief engineer is brutally killed. When informed, Dr. Morbius can only bury his face in his hands. "So it's started again. . . ."

The scientist mysteriously warns them this is only a foretaste: there will be other deaths. The following night precautions are doubled and electronic scanners are placed around the perimeter of the craft. Slow, pounding, footsteps are heard advancing across the dark landscape, but the crew can see nothing. Then, outlined suddenly in the currents of electricity and flares of the blasters, an incredible creature—a huge indefinable beast traced in crackling lightning against the night sky—rears and lunges at the spacemen. Nothing seems to stop the creature. It reaches for two of the crew and vaporizes them. And, just as suddenly, the beast vanishes. . . .

In the Krel laboratory, Morbius has stirred from a terrifying, exhausting nightmare. The circuits behind him are flashing feverishly.

Adams and Doc are dumbfounded. Not even the nuclear disintegrators have stopped the creature. To understand the force they are fighting, Adams reasons, it is important that either he or Doc expose themselves to the IQ-boosting headgear in the Krel lab. They approach Morbius's home; the scientist is nowhere in sight. Robby has been left on guard, but Altaira lets the two spacemen in. While Adams spends a tender moment with the girl (they have fallen in love) Doc makes for the lab entrance.

Time passes. Then Robby lumbers into the room, the spaceman in his arms. Doc's forehead is singed where the headgear's electrodes have touched him. His brain has been enlarged, but mortally damaged. He has, however, discovered the planet's secret. The Krel had completed their project, loosed themselves from the limitations of physical instrumentality and matter,

and escaped into true creation. "But the Krel forgot one thing . . . monsters . . . monsters from the Id. . . ." And Doc dies.

Morbius enters, genuinely shocked at the crewman's death. But then his easy hauteur returns, and he lashes out at Adams for not preventing Doc from meddling. Altaira is repelled by her father's harshness and tells him she wants to leave with the spaceship, to go to Earth. What is the Id? Adams asks. Morbuis, crushed by the turn events have taken, wearily explains it is an obsolete term, "once used to explain the elementary basis of the subconscious mind."

The answer comes to Adams in a flash: the eight thousand miles of underground relays: enough power for a whole population of creative geniuses, operated by remote control, an ultimate machine with power enough to project solid matter anywhere on the planet. "But the Krel forget one deadly danger—their own subconscious hate and lust. And so the mindless beasts of their innermost souls had access to a machine that could never be shut down!" The Krel were all dead—only

their power survived. "After a million years of shining sanity, the Krel could hardly understand the power which was destroying them."

And yet, the scientist counters, there is one fallacy. The Krel died twenty thousand centuries ago, but a monster still stalks this planet today. Adams looks squarely at the older man. "Your mind refuses to accept conclusions." Robby interrupts them; something is coming toward the house; heavy, pounding footsteps can be heard, and the tearing asunder of shrubbery. Morbius immediately activates the

The fantastic subterranean architecture of the Krel (above) to which the earthmen descend with Morbius. In the Krel lab, they project a tiny image of Altaira. Later, they make an impression of the talon of the invisible terror stalking the camp.

heavy steel shutters that form a protective shielding around his house, but he still feels certain that he and his daughter are immune from the creature. But Altaira is not immune, Adams shouts. Love has parted her from her father, and she now belongs to the commander body and soul. "Morbius, when will you face the truth? That thing out there is *you. . . .*"

The force outside comes closer. One of the steel shutters is buckling and melting. Unnerved, the scientist orders Robby to destroy the creature, but the robot has perceived that the force is Morbius's other self. Unable to turn upon his master, the robot fuses itself into immobility. The shutter crumples, and the three make for the underground safety of the Krel lab. The circuits are glowing strangely. Adams forces Morbius to the circuit panels, tells him that through the headgears the older man's subconscious had been strengthened enough to operate the great machines, that nineteen years ago, when Morbius's fellow scientists had voted to return to Earth, "you sent your secret Id out to kill them . . . without realizing it, except maybe in your dreams." The scientist had subconsciously conjured up the terrible power that the Krel first created and that had destroyed them. And now Morbius has summoned this monster again.

The metal thickness shielding the entrance to the lab is white hot, its surface is crystallizing; the force is directly outside. Morbius at last comes to a realization of his guilt; he screams, "Kill him! My evil self is at that door and I have no power to stop it!" The

That night the invisible creature strikes again. This time its outline is etched by the crackling electric barriers and the soldiers' blasters.

gauges across the entire lab, each one ten times the power of the one before it, light up madly. An incredible force is being unleashed. Morbius rushes to the machines. "Stop! *I deny you! I give you up!*" Intense pain registers on his forehead, and with a cry he falls to the floor. The circuits quieten. The burning door shield cools. The force has gone.

Adams and Altaira rush to the scientist. He is dying. He begs the commander to activate a switch, then gasps, "In twenty-four hours you must be a hundred million miles out in space. The Krel furnaces . . . a chain reaction . . . they cannot be reversed. . . ."

Twenty-four hours later, from space, the two lovers watch as Altair IV, with all the stored knowledge of the Krel, explodes, for a moment, into a brief sun. Adams turns to the girl. "About a million years from now the human race will have crawled up to where the Krel stood in their great moment of triumph and tragedy, and your father's name will shine again like a beacon in the galaxy.

MGM had high hopes for *Forbidden Planet,* and yet the initial critical reaction was mixed. Quite a few reviewers were unsettled by a monster from so Freudian a source, evidently preferring—one could read between the lines—a more substantial and traditional adversary. As a result of this reception, MGM scrapped whatever intellectual appeal its advertising was reaching for and concentrated instead on Robby the robot carrying off Altaira in his arms. *Forbidden Planet* drew sizable audiences, but perhaps not the audience it deserved.

For despite its lush, bright, colorful space opera, despite the fact it ends not with a lurid warning but with an embrace, the film is very much a drama of its time. It projects a monster from within ourselves, an enemy to which we

ourselves give birth, destructive forces we ourselves can unknowingly trigger and of which we can be the helpless victim. This suited the temper of the American mid-fifties. MGM had unerringly reflected the very soul of the nation in a classic contribution to the cinema of the fantastic. Strangely enough, the same studio was again to mirror perfectly a later American mood, although with a sharply different and much more subjective film, when in 1968 it released Stanley Kubrick's science fantasy *2001*. And no other studio was to do it sooner.

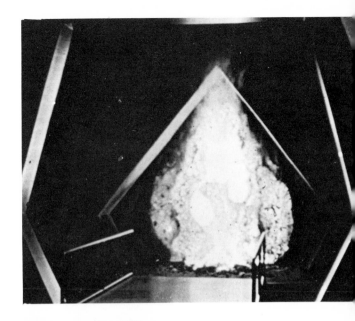

"Morbius, when will you face the truth? That thing out there is *you!*" (far left). An incredible force breaks into the Krel lab, and twenty-four hours later the planet explodes. Bottom picture: a scene deleted from the final film—the wedding of Adams and Altaira.

EPILOGUE

Stanley Kubrick's *2001: A Space Odyssey* is the ultimate vision of the cinema of the fantastic. Not only does it take us on a colossal journey—the beginning of which was first mapped by Méliès—from Earth to an orbiting space station and then to the moon, and farther by rocket freighter across half a million miles of space to the mighty planet Jupiter, and even beyond this outpost on a hair-raising hurtle into other star systems and even other dimensions; we are witness not only to this journey, but also to the evolutionary progress of man. For it is the secret at the core of *2001* that the astronaut played by Keir Dullea does not make his brave, bewildering exploration alone. Rather he symbolizes the whole human race, taking another giant step up the evolutionary ladder to become a species as different from what we are today as we are from the apes clustered at the dawn of time. In each instance the evolutionary acceleration is triggered by the same event: exposure to and intermingling with alien forces, represented in the film as extraterrestrial floating rectangles, monolithic envoys across time and space. For in *2001* the stars are watching across the light years, watching and waiting. . . .

Kubrick's film takes the speculations of the fantastic cinema to a new plateau. The many films that end on a note of relief that mankind remains untouched and unchanged after alien confrontation pale at the vision of *2001,* which climaxes with alien guardians helping mankind to mutate and evolve into an entirely new species better able to meet a destiny out among the stars.

Not all recent examples of the cinema of the fantastic display such dazzling and radical optimism. *Dr. Strangelove*'s war ends civilization. The astronaut landing on *The Planet of the Apes* sees the planet of man in ruins. Yet hope lurks even within the nightmares of desolation and melancholy. Spectacular achievements have been chronicled: the *Fantastic Voyage* through a living human bloodstream. Erotic futures have been chronicled: the lusty triumphs of *Barbarella.* But the most incredible chronicle of all is *2001*, for it brings us to the death and rebirth of humanity itself—and points the way for wonders to come.

282

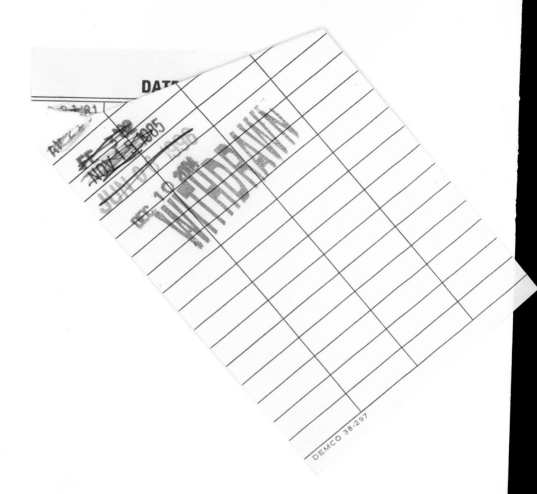